The Door Held

OPEN

The Door Held
OPEN

Reflections on A Course in Miracles

John Cornell

BALBOA.
PRESS

A DIVISION OF HAY HOUSE

ISBN: 978-1-4525-5282-8 (sc)
ISBN: 978-1-4525-5281-1 (e)

Balboa Press books may be ordered through booksellers or by contacting:

Balboa Press
A Division of Hay House
1663 Liberty Drive
Bloomington, IN 47403
www.balboapress.com
1-(877) 407-4847

Because of the dynamic nature of the Internet, any web addresses or links contained in this book may have changed since publication and may no longer be valid. The views expressed in this work are solely those of the author and do not necessarily reflect the views of the publisher, and the publisher hereby disclaims any responsibility for them.

The author of this book does not dispense medical advice or prescribe the use of any technique as a form of treatment for physical, emotional, or medical problems without the advice of a physician, either directly or indirectly. The intent of the author is only to offer information of a general nature to help you in your quest for emotional and spiritual well-being. In the event you use any of the information in this book for yourself, which is your constitutional right, the author and the publisher assume no responsibility for your actions.

Cover photograph Copyright © John Cornell 2012.

Any people depicted in stock imagery provided by Thinkstock are models, and such images are being used for illustrative purposes only. Certain stock imagery © Thinkstock.

Printed in the United States of America

Balboa Press rev. date: 06/28/2012

Joy attends our way. For we go homeward to an open door which God has held unclosed to welcome us.

A Course in Miracles Workbook (Epilogue)

Contents

Note to the reader:

Throughout Part I of the Door Held Open, the original commentaries by John Cornell appear in smaller type just below the quotes from A Course in Miracles. Part II contains passages from A Course in Miracles presented without additional commentary.

Preface

Throughout history people in every age and of every culture have sought to bridge the chasm between the human and the Divine; to find healing for the rift between Man and God. In whatever terms it has been framed, this has been the question, this, the quest. The world's great scriptures and spiritual traditions all address this primary issue in one way or another. Among these spiritual documents and teachings (as well as in rare individuals within almost every tradition) there is a school of thought broadly known as Non-Dualism. The essential teaching is that Reality, although beyond words, is best described as Oneness. In Workbook Lesson 169 *A Course in Miracles* states, "Oneness is simply the idea God is. And in His Being, He encompasses all things." And in chapter 18 we find this radiant proclamation: "Heaven is not a place, nor a condition. It is merely an awareness of perfect Oneness, and the knowledge that there is nothing else; nothing outside this Oneness, and nothing else within."

Although defying classification in many ways, *A Course in Miracles* should be considered a Non-dual teaching. It answers the whole notion of crossing the great divide between Man and God by continually and powerfully reminding us that no such divide is ever even possible.

Introduction

I had become accustomed to glimpsing the title *A Course in Miracles* as I breezed through the "New Age" section of one bookstore or another on my usual pilgrimage to "Eastern Religions." The gold capital letters on a stark navy blue spine always caught my attention, and yet twenty years or more passed by before I so much as peeked inside a copy.

The only thing I had known about the book was that a woman claimed she had received the teachings from a voice that was identified as Jesus! Well, this only served to dampen my curiosity more than ignite it, and with a title like that I had always assumed *A Course in Miracles* was more than likely some shallow program on "how to make cool stuff happen in your life." Not the kind of spirituality I was interested in. I had learned early on, later on, and sometimes the hard way, that there are a lot of paths and teachers, doctrines and disciplines that stop short of true wisdom. There's a lot to see in this amusement park of manifestation, and it's all too easy to believe that some "high" aspect of it is really the goal, really God. It's easy to miss the point.

It was ultimately a book of quotations from the *Course* that afforded me my first actual encounter with this teaching. The smaller, less threatening format and the striking nature photography that accompanied the quotes probably helped me get past my preconceived notions about the book. Several weeks after thus dipping my toe, I knew I wanted to dive deeper, and purchased the Combined Volume, complete edition of *A Course in Miracles*. I was unprepared for what was to follow; months of struggle as I attempted to understand this weighty and wordy document. I frequently found myself asking, "Why in the world would anyone, and Jesus nonetheless, choose to word something so oddly?" Yet amid the difficulty in comprehending what the text was saying, I would at almost every reading, catch some glimmer of real wisdom, some hauntingly beautiful statement on the nature of Reality that would lure me back to its pages again and again. At some point in this process I began to realize that phrases and concepts that had made little or no sense to me previously, were becoming clear. What had seemed to be strange and difficult wording, I now regarded as deeply moving mystical poetry. As this continued the whole teaching started to open up for me, dullard that I am, and I found that this curious and formerly cumbersome document had become my source of daily inspiration and instruction.

I have written the commentaries that appear in Part I in the sincere hope that by closely examining this small handful of passages from the *Course*, readers might find it easier to understand the work in its entirety. It can take time, and in my case quite a bit of patience, to allow this amazing book, this transcendent tome, to reveal itself. In the meantime there is the very real possibility that a number of people who could greatly benefit from this teaching will just throw up their literary hands and walk away. I almost did! It is therefore the aim of this book to decrease the likelihood of such an outcome. Part II presents a sweeping anthology of over 130 quotes from the *Course*, which amount to a veritable manual on life, truth, and our awakening in God. While providing an introduction to *A Course in Miracles* for those just discovering this teaching, *The Door Held Open* is intended to be inspiring and enjoyable reading for long-time students of the *Course* as well.

The sheer size and scope of *A Course in Miracles*, and the vast range of topics it illuminates can make it seem complex. However, the actual beauty of this teaching lies in its simplicity. Truth does not change. Whatever aspect of life we are considering, Christ's message is the same: You are as God created you, and your brothers and sisters along with you.

Origins

The story of how *A Course in Miracles* came into being is a tale of cosmic mystery and of human dedication. What follows is a very brief account of the events that led to the appearance of the *Course*, and of the people who were instrumental. My source for this information is the introduction to *A Course in Miracles,* and the book *Journey Without Distance*, by Robert Skutch.

The year was 1965, and Dr. Helen Schucman was fully occupied in her role as a respected and successful psychologist. While Helen's childhood had been marked by a rather deep interest in spiritual matters, this had long been replaced by an atheistic and thoroughly scientific view of life. As she presently harbored no belief in transcendent wisdom, it goes without saying she had no desire to be the author (by proxy) of a Sacred Text. Her role as "scribe" came about totally unsought and without warning, except for a series of powerful dreams and "unusual experiences" that were a precursor.

Helen's colleague Dr. William Thetford had been struck by the petty, self serving attitudes that prevailed in the psychology department, and having shared his insight with Helen they agreed in no uncertain terms that there must be "another way." The old way wasn't working. Their own professional relationship was strained and difficult, while around them they witnessed captains of academia, pillars of the mental health field, comporting themselves like silly, jealous middle school kids. Neither Bill nor Helen had any idea what this other, better way would be, only that there must be one! Then one day, to her great amazement, Helen heard an inner Voice say, "This is a course in miracles. Please take notes." With a good deal of trepidation, and only after consulting her colleague Bill Thetford, she began to write down what this inner Voice dictated to her. Not even understanding it at first, and certainly not lost in any trance state or blissful reverie, she simply took down what she "heard." She would then read back her shorthand to Dr. Thetford who typed the passages out. This process continued for seven incredible years, gifting the world with the modern scripture we now know as *A Course in Miracles.*

To a jaded philosopher like myself, having witnessed my share of "spiritual" bunk, it comes as a great relief to know that Helen Schucman never saw herself as a religious figure of any kind, and wasn't regarded as such by others. Although never doubting the importance of the material, she didn't claim to exemplify the inner transformation offered in the teachings, and remained bewildered as to why this wisdom had come through her at all. My personal feeling is that it was her very ambivalence to the teaching that made her oddly suited to be the vehicle for its communication. In a curious way, it's as if she didn't "get it," which allowed her to "give it" and not be in the way at all.

Now, the 800 pound gorilla still there munching on Nacho chips in the living room, is whether or not one accepts that the Voice which dictated these teachings is that of Jesus. There are a number of ways to approach this question and just as many ways to answer it. Personally I don't doubt that these are the words of Christ, however, such a conviction is not necessary for the teaching to be of benefit.

Language and the Unutterable Truth

The deepest communication occurs at a level that is free of words and concepts and symbols. Yet, finding ourselves in a world of apparent limitation, we need a form of communication suited to our present state; one that can safely lead us *away* from limitation altogether. Our only real task is to *unlearn* all the illusions we have learned and taught one another thus far. For this, we will still use language and concepts and symbols, never forgetting that they can only take us up to the stepping off point, where truth itself becomes the teaching, and the wordless vision of God's Unity replaces every word and symbol and concept.

While studying *A Course in Miracles,* it is important not to become bogged down by any specific phrase or term that one may find off-putting in some way. For example, the exclusive use of the masculine form throughout the *Course* is intended to point beyond questions of gender, not to suggest that deep down everybody's a boy, or that God is ultimately male. Workbook Lesson 184 sheds a good deal of light on the matter of language and its limitations as well as its usefulness. "Learning that stops with what the world would teach stops short of meaning. In its proper place, it serves but as a starting point from which another kind of learning can begin, a new perception can be gained, and all the arbitrary names the world bestows can be withdrawn as they are raised to doubt." "It would indeed be strange if you were asked to go beyond all symbols of the world, forgetting them forever; yet were asked to take a teaching function. You have need to use the symbols of the world a while. But be you not deceived by them as well. They do not stand for anything at all, and in your practicing it is this thought that will release you from them. They become but means by which you can communicate in ways the world can understand, but which you recognize is not the unity where true communication can be found."

It is with this understanding that we can encounter any seeming contradictions within the *Course's* pages, and realize that these represent lessons, not lapses in consistency. A concept that serves as a useful symbol at one time will bring us even greater light when, in due time, it is allowed to fall away. As a case in point, there are numerous passages in which the *Course* uses the image of a journey; of moving along a road. Yet in the thirteenth chapter we are told, "...there is no journey, but only an awakening." Also, " There is no road to travel on, and no time to travel through. For God waits not for His Son in time, being forever unwilling to be without him." These are not contradictions at all, but clarifications of the teaching. So let us keep in mind the inherently feeble nature of every symbol and concept, never allowing their dim shadow to obscure the shining of truth's transforming light.

Again Lesson 184 spells it out clearly. "Use all the little names and symbols which delineate the world of darkness. Yet accept them not as your reality. The Holy Spirit uses all of them, but He does not forget creation has one Name, one meaning, and a single Source which unifies all things within Itself. Use all the names the world bestows on them but for convenience, yet do not forget they all share the Name of God along with you." This passage from Lesson 122 serves as a fitting close to our brief discussion of the role and the limits of language as a vehicle for truth. "Open your eyes today and look upon a happy world of safety and of peace. Forgiveness is the means by which it comes to take the place of hell. In quietness it rises up to greet your open eyes, and fill your heart with deep tranquility as ancient truths, forever newly born, arise in your awareness. What you will remember then can never be described. Yet your forgiveness offers it to you."

The *Course*, the Cross, and True Forgiveness

One need not look far to find passionate and vocal critics of *A Course in Miracles* who claim that while it poses as Christianity, it is something entirely different and therefore heretical and dangerous. It should be remembered that those who make such statements generally believe that anything other than their own brand of religion is, in fact, heresy. *A Course in Miracles* will obviously not sit well with this type of theologian. After all, nobody's eternally burning in hell here, and where's the fun in that? In fairness to its critics however, I would actually agree that the *Course* is not a traditional Christian teaching. Yet truth be told, it never claims to be. In the introduction to *A Course in Miracles,* the teaching is described as "one version of the universal curriculum." This is a universal teaching for an age that *needs* just that. The fact that the *Course* presents a view of the crucifixion and the resurrection which differs from the commonly held interpretation is a call for reason and thoughtful, prayerful consideration, not blind rejection and condemnation.

In the theology of *A Course in Miracles*, crucifixion is what *sin* brings to the table. Crucifixion itself is the very image, the archetype of how the ego and its thought system interpret and administer justice. It's the pinnacle of hatred, shown to all of us in stark and brutal clarity. The sinful, separate ego offers crucifixion and death to any part of life that stands in its way. Look around you; humanity caught in the grip of greed, oppression, and violence. None of this is God's will. It's merely what we have projected and made manifest in our *forgetfulness* of God.

Only love can be regarded as an expression of God's will. The Love our Heavenly Father has for us is eternal, and does not change. Therefore, Christ's resurrection and his offering of forgiveness in the face of crucifixion was the *demonstration* of that eternal Love and mercy, *not* the creation of it. Put simply, the heart of the story isn't that Jesus died for our sins it's that he didn't die. The resurrection is the glorious sign that sin is without power to affect God's beloved Son or to thwart God's will, which *is* eternal life. The resurrection is God's answer to the crucifixion. Love is God's unfailing response to hate. Forgiveness is His sentence on the guilty...this is the message of Christ.

The world offers the first part; the murderous part. God settles the matter by teaching us that condemnation and death are powerless to destroy What is eternal. The changeless and all-forgiving nature of God's Love is Christ's only message to a world tormented by pain, guilt, and needless despair.

In the thirteenth chapter of *A Course in Miracles*, we find these revealing passages. "Easter is not the celebration of the *cost* of sin, but of its *end*." "There *is* no fear in love. The song of Easter is the glad refrain the Son of God was never crucified. Let us lift up our eyes together, not in fear but faith. And there will be no fear in us, for in our vision will be no illusions; only a pathway to the open door of Heaven, the home we share in quietness and where we live in gentleness and peace, as one together."

There is no time, no place, no state where God
is absent. There is nothing to be feared.

God's Presence, which is Love, remains the truth despite all evidence to the contrary. Reality remains intact. Every perceived state, thought or action that is not love, is at its heart an expression of fear. Fear is the inevitable outcome of not seeing love; not acknowledging the truth. Nonetheless, it is vitally important to remember that God's eternal Presence does not ever, nor in any way, *cease to be* merely because we lack vision.

An analogy will help to make this easily understood. Consider the case of that catch-all chair you have in your bedroom. You clutter it and pile all manner of clothes and such on it 'til you can no longer see the chair at all. But the chair is still there. In the same way, God's Presence remains constant and undiminished despite all the dark and fearful obstructions we have trained ourselves to see instead. There *is* nothing to be feared.

You cannot separate your Self from your Creator,
Who created you by sharing His Being with you.

Chapter 7 V: 6 (15)

Thoughts do not leave their source. This is a principle absolutely central to understanding the teaching we receive in *A Course in Miracles*. We can and do experience the totally convincing sensation of separation from God, but that doesn't make the separation factual in any way. We are all thoughts in the Mind of God, and we have not left our Source. The beautiful realizations that arise from this simple statement of wisdom are indeed endless. Workbook Lesson 164 gives us this passage: "There is a silence into which the world can not intrude. There is an ancient peace you carry in your heart and have not lost. There is a sense of holiness in you the thought of sin has never touched." This is our natural state of Grace; our eternal inheritance from the Father. All seemingly separate selves are united in Truth, joined forever in the Oneness of Everlasting Life. We are all the One Self, the very Son of God.

Remember always that you cannot be anywhere
except in the Mind of God. When you forget
this, you *will* despair and you *will* attack.

Chapter 9 VIII: 5 (3-4)

Only God *is*. Only truth is true. We have sprung forth in the Mind of God and we abide there still. There is, literally nowhere else to go. We can seem to make a dream world, and imagine it to be peopled with so-called "others," but the *fact* of our union and of our identity as the Son of God, remains the only truth. The *Course* reminds us over and over that dreams are powerless to alter reality. Truth is forever true, regardless of what form illusion takes. It is only in this dream of separation that our nightmares of guilt, fear, and suffering are experienced. In the midst of our 3-D dream dilemma, it seems we inevitably find ourselves oppressed by relentless forces that would destroy us, and lashing out at them in a vain attempt at finding safety and peace. Unaware that we exist *in* God, we despair and we attack.

It is sobering and yet somehow oddly reassuring that the first sentence in this quote begins with "Remember always" and the second sentence with "When you forget this." The world we see every day is a blazing testament to what expert forgetters we are. Our seeing has stopped short of vision, and so (for the most part) we perceive and experience and offer one another only the world as forgetfulness pictures it. In our spiritual amnesia we see and reflect an image distorted, unclear, and unworthy of the truth that is our real and eternally shared Identity in God.

When you made visible what is not true,
what *is* true became invisible to you.

Chapter 12 VIII: 3 (1)

Truth is highly inconvenient and even unintelligible from the ego's perspective. So much so that it elected to adopt another, more suitable version of reality to replace the truth. Now of course nothing can ever actually replace the truth. By definition, truth is always true. Therefore the ego's attempt at redefining reality is a concept without meaning; an endeavor without possibility of accomplishment. However, perception is concerned only with what it *sees,* not with what *is,* and the ego's frame of reference is built solely on perception. It remains entirely oblivious of the truth as knowledge would reveal it.

The split mind (ego) sees division, conflict, and the mere "fact" of bodily existence as proof that the grandeur of God is nonexistent and Heaven is but a dream. It's as if we're standing at the brink of eternity, witness to the spectacular vista of God's endless Kingdom, and we are *imagining* instead that we're stranded in some gloomy bus station. We've traded eternity itself for the pitiful trinkets time had to offer. There is a wonderful line in *Walden* that captures our predicament. "We now no longer camp as for a night, but have settled down on Earth and forgotten Heaven."

If you will lay aside the ego's voice, however loudly
it may seem to call; if you will not accept its petty
gifts that give you nothing that you really want;
if you will listen with an open mind, that has not
told you what salvation is; then you will hear the
mighty Voice of truth, quiet in power, strong in
stillness, and completely certain in Its messages.

Workbook Lesson 106: 1 (1)

Most of us live like members of a captive audience, trapped in the darkened theater of our own minds, listening without interruption to the ego's meaningless grievances, goals, and strategies. We decided long ago in our self-defined and limited state, that we know what's best. We have therefore set the agenda and are reaping the "benefits" of our choice; a never ending episode of "Lifestyles of the Wounded and Universally Discontent." Untold time and energy has been wasted pursuing the worthless "gifts" of the ego. It never seems to occur to us that we have the option of choosing a different program, of listening to a voice not clamoring for our attention; a Voice that is constant, true, and already present in full and unambiguous clarity.

You can't really begin to ignore the ego's fearful message until you know that it's got nothing to offer you. The version of reality the ego would have you subscribe to is not reality at all. Look squarely at what the ego has made, and see where this split mind has gotten us: Fear, mistrust, oppression, violence, and a looming global environmental disaster we couldn't have imagined a few short, arrogant decades ago. The world chose the voice it would follow, and the results are undeniable.

It's not the case however, that truth does not speak to us. Rather than through a barrage of sounds, and symbols, and partial meanings, it speaks in the silent and timeless language of eternal Oneness. Far from being mute or obscure, Truth Itself is indeed the only Voice there is to hear if we can lay aside the ego's incessant yammering.

Forgiveness lets the veil be lifted up that hides the
face of Christ from those who look with unforgiving
eyes upon the world. It lets you recognize the
Son of God, and clears your memory of all dead
thoughts so that remembrance of your Father
can arise across the threshold of your mind.

Workbook Lesson 122: 3 (1-2)

This relatively brief quote reflects the essence of *A Course in Miracles*.
This is the heart of the matter, the crux of the biscuit if you will.
Forgiveness sees beyond illusion, making way for real vision. There is in
truth One Self, the Christ, and we are *all,* that One. Until this Oneness
becomes our frame of reference and our firm foundation, we will simply
continue to act out the dramas of guilt, denial, and death. It sure ain't
pretty, but that's the way it is.

To hold an image of the past, of guilt and sinfulness, as being
the truth of your brothers and sisters, is to lose of sight them as they
were created by God. And failing to recognize the light in them,
it's impossible that you could behold it in yourself. Real forgiveness
removes the barrier to true vision by seeing nothing but the truth as
true. Only the holiness in which God created us has any validity. The
rest is a nightmare we trade back and forth with our fellow beings,
obscuring our awareness that we are One in Christ, united everlastingly
with the Father.

Each one you see you place within the holy circle
of Atonement or leave outside, judging him fit for
crucifixion or for redemption. If you bring him into
the circle of purity, you will rest there with him. If
you leave him without, you join him there. Judge not
except in quietness which is not of you. Refuse to
accept anyone as without the blessing of Atonement,
and bring him into it by blessing him. Holiness must
be shared, for therein lies everything that makes it
holy. Come gladly to the holy circle, and look out in
peace on all who think they are outside. Cast no one
out, for here is what he seeks along with you. Come,
let us join him in the holy place of peace which is for
all of us, united as one within the Cause of peace.

Chapter 14 V: 11 (1-9)

There is no salvation, no awareness of Oneness, for any mind that would attempt to exclude any "other" mind *from* this Oneness. The only ticket into the holy circle of God's peace is to see your brothers and sisters abiding there with you. To cast anyone out is to *be* cast out because there is only one of us. We are either forgiven or we are condemned, all as one. As it turns out, we *are* forgiven. So, do not judge anyone based on your own petty and shifting perceptions. Look instead to the peace of God in you; that deep quietness of Being that is not of your making. To behold another as sinless is to see your own innocence as well. And seeing this, you will offer and receive only this, for only *this* is true.

7

The betrayal of the Son of God lies only in illusions,
and all his "sins" are but his own imagining. His
reality is forever sinless. He need not be forgiven but
awakened. In his dreams he has betrayed himself, his
brothers and his God. Yet what is done in dreams
has not been really done. It is impossible to convince
the dreamer that this is so, for dreams are what
they are *because* of their illusion of reality. Only in
waking is the full release from them, for only then
does it become perfectly apparent that they had no
effect upon reality at all, and did not change it.

Chapter 17 I: 1 (1-7)

The best way out of a disaster is to suddenly realize that it never happened. It goes without saying that the history of humankind is a rather tragic, murderous, and greedy tale. Yet God's true and certain verdict is that His Son is blameless, despite the crimes he thinks he has committed. Our sinless reality, our Self as created by God, is eternally changeless and unscathed by all the apparent abuses of this world. In your dreams you may find yourself held captive by bloodthirsty pirates, or sitting quietly in a lovely garden sipping tea. However, from the point of view of wakefulness it is entirely obvious that neither one has happened at all.

It may be very difficult, or at times seemingly impossible, to see through this dream life and become aware of reality *as it is*, free of illusion. Within the dream we seldom ever even question if the dream is real. Yet that is exactly the purpose of this course, the purpose of this life. Reality Itself is our salvation and the undoing of illusion. Wakefulness brings the end of dreaming, and with it, "forgiveness" for what was never really done.

The happy dreams the Holy Spirit brings are different
from the dreaming of the world, where one can merely
dream he is awake. The dreams forgiveness lets the
mind perceive do not induce another form of sleep,
so that the dreamer dreams another dream. His happy
dreams are heralds of the dawn of truth upon the
mind. They lead from sleep to gentle waking, so that
dreams are gone. And thus they cure for all eternity.

Lesson 140: 3 (1-5)

Truth is always and only Oneness with God; the full waking state of
Heaven's endless joy. All else, as we have said, is the stuff of dreams.
However, there are dreams that lead us to deeper sleep and yet more
dreaming, and there are "happy dreams" that lead to awakening. Dreams
of faith and forgiveness lead to waking, whereas dreams of vengeance
lead to still more nightmares of hatred, fear, and separation. The giving
and receiving of forgiveness *within* the dream removes the painful clench
that makes it all seem real in the first place.

The *Course* is very clear in stating that forgiveness itself is but a
dream. Yet it is a dream that leads beyond all dreaming at last, revealing
to us the eternal truth wherein no one ever *needed* forgiveness. Thus,
forgiveness is the final form the dream takes before we are brought to
wakefulness. The happy dreams the Holy Spirit offers gently awaken us
to Heaven, Where we have always remained and Where our sleeping
never entered in.

There is nothing you can hold against reality. All
that must be forgiven are the illusions you have
held against your brothers. Their reality has no
past, and only illusions can be forgiven. God holds
nothing against anyone, for He is incapable of
illusions of any kind. Release your brothers from
the slavery of their illusions by forgiving them
for the illusions you perceive in them. Thus will
you be forgiven, for it is you who offered them
illusions. In the holy instant this is done for you in
time, to bring you the true condition of Heaven.

Chapter 16 VII: 9 (1-7)

What is the "true condition of Heaven?" Peace. Holiness. Love
unending. In a word, Oneness with God. This is the truth, forever
untainted, pure, and complete. This timeless Reality is the truth of you
and of everyone else. This is the "you" God created and the only one
He knows. The rest of it, whatever you want to call it, is illusory and
therefore nonexistent.

The only possible release from illusion is truth itself, and that which
is true *needs* no forgiveness. Therefore, to forgive truly is simply to offer
another the gift of being seen free of guilt, holy as he or she was created.
And as we offer true forgiveness we receive it as well. Not because one
act or attitude engenders the other, but because they are one and the
same. Forgiveness takes place in any single moment which is released
and left only to God's undivided purpose. The holy instant gives us a
taste, in time, of our timeless and eternal home in Heaven.

Projection makes perception, and you cannot see beyond it. Again and again you have attacked your brother, because you saw in him a shadow figure in your private world. And thus it is you must attack yourself first, for what you attack is not in others. Its only reality is in your own mind, and by attacking others you are literally attacking what is not there.

Chapter 13 V: 3 (5-8)

The idea that what we perceive is our own projection is a difficult concept to come to terms with. We have been in the full time business of placing guilt on our fellow beings, letting blame rest anywhere but on our own heads. All of this comes as "naturally" to us as breathing. Our inner world has been constructed from illusory building blocks, and inhabited by characters of our own invention. We assign roles to the people we encounter, and we react to them based on our own private version of reality. If we could see beyond the level of our projection, to the truth that resides in everyone, there would be no question of attack or blame. There would be only blessing, and love without limit.

It's important to point out that the *Course* is not teaching that everyone other than you is an illusion, and not really there. The truth is that we have yet to *see* the truth, and therefore what we are attacking is a villain we ourselves concocted; a monster we cooked up in the basement, so to speak. If we had not first believed ourselves to be an ego, which is an attack on our own true Self, we would effortlessly see beyond the mask of illusion we've placed on our fellow beings as well.

Christ's vision has one law. It does not look upon a
body, and mistake it for the Son whom God created. It
beholds a light beyond the body; an idea beyond what
can be touched, a purity undimmed by errors, pitiful
mistakes, and fearful thoughts of guilt from dreams of
sin. It sees no separation. And it looks on everyone,
on every circumstance, all happenings and all events,
without the slightest fading of the light it sees.

Workbook Lesson 158: 7 (1-5)

Our way of seeing is, spiritually speaking, a form of blindness. We rely on boundaries, distinctions and differences as the very fabric of our awareness, yet all of this pertains to the world of darkness and is not real seeing at all. The vision Christ would give to us, the vision of our true Self, does not look to limitation for the Answer. True vision transcends the entire context of separation, seeing only the one eternal light in which shadows make no difference at all. This light is our heritage and our home, remaining forever untouched by such notions as "the body," "sin," and "death."

The following words from the text of *A Course in Miracles* clarify beautifully this distinction between the two ways of seeing that are available to us. In fact, this passage clarifies the whole shootin' match, ultimately pointing beyond seeing, beyond all perception, to our joyous reunion in the Heart of God. "Do not seek vision through your eyes, for you made your way of seeing that you might see in darkness, and in this you are deceived. Beyond this darkness, and yet still within you, is the vision of Christ, Who looks on all in light. Your "vision" comes from fear, as His from love. And He sees for you, as your witness to the real world. He is the Holy Spirit's manifestation, looking always on the real world, and calling forth its witnesses and drawing them to you. He loves what He sees within you, and He would extend it. And He will not return unto the Father until He has extended your perception even unto Him. And there perception is no more, for He has returned you to the Father with Him."

Seek ye first the Kingdom of Heaven, because that
is where the laws of God operate truly, and they
can operate only truly because they are the laws of
truth. But seek this only for you can find nothing
else. There *is* nothing else. God is All in all in a very
literal sense. All being is in Him Who is all Being.
You are therefore in Him since your being is His.

Chapter 7 IV: 7 (1-6)

The joy we fail to find in this dusty world is ours nonetheless. However,
we can never be content with *anything* that is less than *everything*. Which
is to say, only the Oneness of Heaven can be home for us; only the
unending joy of God's Being will bring us fulfillment. Yet there is no
cause for alarm. We will know the joy of God, for there *is* nothing
else to know. We will *be* in Heaven, because in truth that is where we
already are.

The ego can accept the idea that return is necessary
because it can so easily make the idea seem difficult.
Yet the Holy Spirit tells you that even return
is unnecessary, because what never happened
cannot be difficult. However, you can *make* the
idea of return both necessary and difficult. Yet it
is surely clear that the perfect need nothing, and
you cannot experience perfection as a difficult
accomplishment, because that is what you are.

Chapter 6 II: 11 (1-4)

All this talk of Heaven, and the longing we feel for our reunion in God, is a genuine expression of truth. But like absolutely everything else, the ego can get a hold of it and turn it into an ego trip. The ego will always present you with a ladder, a stairway to heaven, a yellow brick road of some kind. It may be in the form of past and future lives, or of chakras, and energies, and various planes of awareness. It may simply be the notion of moving through time toward a goal, a God, or a moral station not yet present. All of this, as true as it may be, is only true from the ego's point of view. How can we return to God when we never left? How can you achieve perfection, when you've never been anything else? When we hear the Holy Spirit's assessment of the situation, all the sense of climbing, of reaching and striving for truth gives way to Truth Itself. And the truth is that we never left God. Our perfection was never in jeopardy. When Dorothy got back to Kansas, the real glory of it all, the truly joyful thing, was that she never really left.

Under all the senseless thoughts and mad ideas
with which you have cluttered up your mind are
the thoughts that you thought with God in the
beginning. They are there in your mind now,
completely unchanged. They will always be in
your mind, exactly as they always were. Everything
you have thought since then will change, but the
Foundation on which it rests is wholly changeless.

Workbook Lesson 45: 7 (1-4)

Our mental chaos; all of our ups and downs, and ins and outs, have not tarnished reality. We have been, and we will forever be, unable to obstruct God's Presence despite the full force of human insanity. We were endowed with the thoughts of God, with an awareness of truth, in our very creation. This joyous knowledge is our ancient and unalterable Foundation. What is eternal is changeless and is therefore always present, always *now*. Thus it is we carry eternity with us through time until we lay time itself aside in the knowledge that eternity is all that ever was.

The reflections you accept into the mirror of your
mind in time but bring eternity nearer or farther. But
eternity itself is beyond all time. Reach out of time
and touch it, with the help of its reflection in you.

Chapter 14 X: 1 (2-4)

We don't have to trek out and find eternity, because eternity is reflected right within us. That Which is eternal shines unobstructed as the deepest truth of who we are. We can become distracted for a time by the fleeting images that play across the surface and convince us that the truth is no longer true. However, it must be said once again, truth is *always* true. It would be a daunting task for certain if we had to actually make it from point A to point B; if we had to journey from time to eternity. Yet it is the light of eternity itself that frees us from time, vanishing all reflections in the overwhelming glow of God's endless Being.

The response of holiness to any form of error is
always the same. There is no contradiction in what
holiness calls forth. Its one response is healing,
without regard for what is brought to it. Those
who have learned to offer only healing, because of
the reflection of holiness in them, are ready at last
for Heaven. There, holiness is not a reflection, but
rather the actual condition of what was but reflected
to them here. God is no image, and His creations,
as part of Him, hold Him in them in truth. They
do not merely reflect truth, for they *are* truth.

Chapter 14 IX: 8 (1-7)

Error takes countless forms but it's really always the same error. Whatever else it may appear to be for the time being, it is ultimately the projection and the experience of suffering, separation, and the loss of wholeness. Healing also appears to take a variety of forms, but it always involves the *restoring* of wholeness to minds that believe wholeness has been lost. God's reflection within us, which is holiness, invariably offers healing in the face of whatever error it encounters. This is because only healing will help. It is only the awareness of wholeness that can cause the experience of separation and suffering to disappear. This is totally unlike the ego's approach to the situation. In the ego's world, one error might call for a thoughtful word of correction, and another might lead to someone getting punched in the nose!

When we have learned that God's reflection in us is our only reality, and that this same reflection, pure and complete, is the only reality of our fellow beings, we are at last beginning to see beyond this error-stricken world. What is merely reflected here has its shining Source in Heaven Itself. We are all in and of God entirely. The light given to us as our true and shared Identity is God's own brightness, eternal and undivided.

In time, the Holy Spirit clearly sees the Son of God
can make mistakes. On this you share His vision. Yet
you do not share His recognition of the difference
between time and eternity. And when correction is
completed, time *is* eternity. The Holy Spirit can teach
you how to look on time differently and see beyond
it, but not while you believe in sin. In error, yes, for
this can be corrected by the mind. But sin is the belief
that your perception is unchangeable, and that the
mind must accept as true what it is told through it.

Chapter 19 III: 5 (1-7)

The Holy Spirit is the inner Teacher; the One within each of us Who
sees the truth *for us* when we have yet to see it ourselves. At present, our
way of "seeing" bears little resemblance to the Holy Spirit's vision except
that both agree mistakes have been, and are being made. However, what
the Holy Spirit sees as error, the ego regards as sin; solid, immoveable,
and incapable of correction. We look on the irrefutable evidence that
all these countless errors and infractions exist, and this becomes the sum
total of our "vision." An error or mistake that takes place in time, as
they *all* do, is viewed as sin when we are unable to see *beyond* time, into
eternity. As we learn to accept the Holy Spirit's vision as our own, we
free ourselves and all our fellow beings from the unbearable burden of
time and all its "sinful" implications.

To "single out" is to "make alone," and thus make lonely. God did not do this to you. Could He set you apart, knowing that your peace lies in His Oneness?

Chapter 13 III: 12 (1-3)

We find ourselves huddled here in time, feeling abandoned by our Creator, alone in a dark and threatening universe. Hogwash! We weren't *cast* out of the Garden; we ducked out for a smoke and have wandered way too deep into guilt, attack, and self-pity to ever want to show our face again. It may be a tough pill to swallow, but at some point we have to take responsibility for the separation. After all, it wasn't God's idea. The separation and the shattering of peace, was not done *to* us, but rather *by* us. In chapter 27 (VIII: 6) we read this stirring account of our situation: "Into eternity, where all is one, there crept a tiny, mad idea, at which the Son of God remembered not to laugh. In his forgetting did the thought become a serious idea, and possible of both accomplishment and real effects. Together we can laugh them both away, and understand that time cannot intrude upon eternity." Both the separation and the world of effects that it brings about are of our own doing. And being based on a faulty perception, an untrue thought system, they are insubstantial; no more than nothingness really. A dreadful and terrifying world has seemingly arisen from what should have been greeted as a mere pun or a silly knock-knock joke. The Oneness that is our Source, and that is God's eternal Will for us, is forever the only reality.

To be alone is to be separated from infinity, but
how can this be if infinity has no end? No one can
be beyond the limitless, because what has no limits
must be everywhere. There are no beginnings and
no endings in God, Whose universe is Himself. Can
you exclude yourself from the universe, or from God
Who *is* the universe? I and my Father are one with
you, for you are part of Us. Do you really believe
that part of God can be missing or lost to Him?

Chapter 11 I: 2 (1-6)

Patiently, consistently, and with great gladness the *Course* reminds us that there is nowhere to go other than the very Being of God, where, as it turns out, we have always been. Infinity, by definition, is all encompassing and therefore everywhere, and always present. However, when we lose the awareness and the knowledge that our own being is part of infinite and eternal Being, we experience limitation in the form of fear, anxiety, depression, and loneliness. As human beings we are unfortunately a good deal more familiar with these various sates of fear and isolation than we are with the bliss of infinity. Nonetheless, the memory and the sense of limitlessness are there in each and every one of us, waiting only to be reawakened.

An insightful and precocious little five year old girl once asked, as she was being tucked in for the night, "Did you ever think that all of this is just a dream?" And her equally precocious younger brother, also at about that same age, posed this metaphysical conundrum, "What if there wasn't anything; no world, no people, no air, no stars, (and leaning forward, as he placed his thumb and forefinger close together in the universal symbol of "just a smidgen," he whispered) and not even one little thing of thunder?" From the mouth of babes. These honest and unvarnished statements reflect an innate and clear remembrance of our Blissful Homeland; our native state of union with God. At the deepest level we all know that Reality is the unending joy of limitless Being, but at some point we've become convinced otherwise. Just beneath the illusory thoughts and

perceptions we cling to in desperation, lie the joyous memory of our limitless Origin and our eternal oneness with the Father in Christ. "Could any part of God be without His Love, and could any part of His Love be contained? God is your heritage, because His one gift is Himself." Chapter 11 I: 7 (1-2)

Each day, and every minute in each day, and every
instant that each minute holds, you but relive the single
instant when the time of terror took the place of love.

Chapter 26 V: 13 (1)

Our apparent fall from the Arms of Infinite Love onto the hard, cold, linoleum of separation was a shock we have yet to recover from. The whole of humanity is suffering from a classic case of post-traumatic stress disorder. We have been overcome with fear and terminal uncertainty since the moment Heaven's peace was shattered. In that very first instant, when we imagined that guilt had become real and that eternal Oneness had been abandoned, we wrote the tune we would be dancing to throughout all the ages that followed. To this day our perception and our experience are completely dependent on, and distorted by, this persistent, self-inflicted "wound." A few sentences further in the text the voice of Christ reveals the simple remedy for all this fear and pain and senseless confusion: "Forgive the past and let it go, for it *is* gone." If we simply become willing to offer and accept release from the pain of this alleged and ancient split, we find there is no longer any foundation on which to *build* conditions of pain and separation in the present. This is the miracle of forgiveness, given and received.

The tiny tick of time in which the first mistake was
made, and all of them within that one mistake, held
also the Correction for that one, and all of them
that came within the first. And in that tiny instant
time was gone, for that was all it ever was. What
God gave answer to is answered and is gone.

Chapter 26 V: 3 (5-7)

The moment we experienced the separation, God's answer was already
in place. "It never happened." Reality has a safety mechanism built right
in, and it's this; that for all our abilities as the Son of God, we are not
able to make real what cannot be. Therefore, as God did not will that
His Oneness be lost, It remains intact. The entire spectacle of time and
the vast cosmic drama we see around us, are like the recurring memory
of a mistake that has already been corrected. Because we've remained
oblivious to God's answer, we thrash about like frantic numerals in an
equation to which the solution has never really been unknown.

A Course in Miracles gives us a wealth of wisdom concerning that
initial mistake; the "catastrophic" moment when all hell broke loose.
The vivid and moving account which follows is but one of many: "The
tiny instant you would keep and make eternal, passed away in Heaven
too soon for anything to notice it had come. What disappeared too
quickly to affect the simple knowledge of the Son of God can hardly
still be there, for you to choose to be your teacher. Only in the past,-an
ancient past, too short to make a world in answer to creation,-did this
world appear to rise. So very long ago, for such a tiny interval of time,
that not one note in Heaven's song was missed. Yet in each unforgiving
act or thought, in every judgment and in all belief in sin, is that one
instant still called back, as if it could be made again in time. You keep an
ancient memory before your eyes. And he who lives in memories alone
is unaware of where he is." Again Christ's words offer us assurance that
there is nothing to be feared. "Forget the time of terror that has been so
long ago corrected and undone. Can sin withstand the Will of God?"

Forgiveness is the great release from time. It is the
key to learning that the past is over. Madness speaks
no more. There *is* no other teacher and no other
way. For what has been undone no longer is.

Chapter 26 V: 6 (1-5)

Forgiveness, truly offered and received, shows us unfailingly that the past is past. What has been undone is gone and does not exist. Such it is with everything, all the way back to our "fall from grace" and our alleged separation from God. It was answered and is no more. You see, we may have forgotten to laugh at the "mad idea" of separation, but the Almighty has never *stopped* laughing. And in His boundless laughter, madness is forever silenced. Only forgiveness opens the door to truth and provides a way to freedom, by teaching us that Heaven's Oneness was never really sacrificed.

You maker of a world that is not so, take rest and
comfort in another world where peace abides. This
world you bring with you to all the weary eyes and
tired hearts that look on sin and beat its sad refrain.
From you can come their rest. From you can rise a
world they will rejoice to look upon, and where their
hearts are glad. In you there is a vision that extends to
all of them, and covers them in gentleness and light.
And in this widening world of light the darkness they
thought was there is pushed away, until it is but distant
shadows, far away, not long to be remembered as the
sun shines them to nothingness. And all their "evil"
thoughts and "sinful" hopes, their dreams of guilt and
merciless revenge, and every wish to hurt and kill
and die, will disappear before the sun you bring.

Chapter 25 IV: 3 (1-7)

We are always free to lay aside this illusion of a world we have worked
so diligently to construct. The ego's version of reality is *not* reality,
and knowing this can come to be our greatest comfort, and the source
of unending peace. For so long now we have been peering at one
another through the cracked and clouded goggles of "sin," accepting
a distorted perception of reality in which we suffer the brutal injustice
of a darkened world. The truth is that Reality is inherently blissful,
and Eternal Existence is the very nature of life. Yet this world's weary
inhabitants have become the confused, vengeful, and desperate victims
of their own hopeless vision of the universe.

In the midst of this pain and isolation they long for the peace of a higher
world; a peace you can offer them. You see beyond this world, or you surely
will by this time next Tuesday, and so you bring with you to this world the
graceful beneficence of the world of light. The gentle offering of Heaven's
peace is the only gift this wounded and dying world requires. To behold
this light is to see it shining everywhere, always, in everyone, and to watch
in wordless joy as it dissolves every lingering trace of darkness.

In you is all of Heaven. Every leaf that falls is given
life in you. Each bird that ever sang will sing again in
you. And every flower that ever bloomed has saved
its perfume and its loveliness for you. What aim can
supersede the Will of God and of His Son, that Heaven
be restored to him for whom it was created as his only
home? Nothing before and nothing after it. No other
place; no other state nor time. Nothing beyond nor
nearer. Nothing else. In any form. This can you bring
to all the world, and all the thoughts that entered it
and were mistaken for a little while. How better could
your own mistakes be brought to truth than by your
willingness to bring the light of Heaven with you, as
you walk beyond the world of darkness into light?

Chapter 25 IV: 5 (1-12)

Nothing is ever lost. All the beauty and loveliness we have seen and
felt and known in this world are not to be wrested from us. As truth
begins to take the fore in our awareness it is only illusion that falls away,
revealing to us what has *always* been true. The ineffable totality of God
and the Heaven of His limitless Being are beyond our ability to accept
or reject. Our oneness with Reality, being the Will of God, is not a
matter of debate. It is the simple truth, the only Fact.

There are innumerable dreams being experienced at any given
moment. A separate version of the universe is presented to each mind
that still believes itself to be separate. Nevertheless, no mind is ever
really separate. No one is ever alone. The Absolute and unspeakable
joy that is God's Presence is our very home. We live in God now. This
timeless joy of life and the unifying vision of What eternally Is, leaves us
no room for any thought or action that is less than love. In the presence
of light, shadows can not endure. Thus we reach a point at which
illusion simply feels unnatural, and we are uncomfortable harboring
thoughts of judgment and condemnation of any kind.

As we choose to offer one another freedom from the pain of separation instead of still *more* separation, we will turn together and walk into the eternal light that had ceased to shine only in our darkened imaginations. "And in the sunlight you will stand in quiet, in innocence and wholly unafraid. And from you will the rest you found extend, so that your peace can never fall away and leave you homeless. Those who offer peace to everyone have found a home in Heaven the world cannot destroy. For it is large enough to hold the world within its peace." Chapter 25 IV: 4 (7-10)

You *will* undertake a journey because you are not at home in this world. And you *will* search for your home whether you realize where it is or not. If you believe it is outside of you the search will be futile, for you will be seeking it where it is not. You do not remember how to look within for you do not believe your home is there. Yet the Holy Spirit remembers it for you, and He will guide you to your home because that is His mission. As He fulfills His mission He will teach you yours, for your mission is the same as His. By guiding your brothers home you are but following Him.

Chapter 12 IV: 5 (1-7)

It may not appear to be the case, but everyone in this world is seeking the same thing. All of the adventures and exploits, the triumphs and trials of humankind, have arisen in the wake of our search for the native bliss of Being. Because absolute Oneness is our home, we will never be able to find rest or fulfillment in a harsh and fractured world of finite dimensions. But by God we're going to try! And so it is we've scoured the landscape, searching everywhere for what it is not to be found in the outside world at all. We've racked up millions of miles, as it were, on a scooter that could have just as well stayed in the driveway.

So many ages have been spent in this fruitless scavenger hunt; we no longer remember how to turn our gaze within. Yet it is inward vision alone that can see beyond the facade of this world, reawakening our memory of the Home we never left. Our ever present inner Guide, the Holy Spirit, has never forgotten our eternal connection to reality; our Oneness with God. As we are led away from the illusory world of separation, we join the Holy Spirit in bringing all living beings to share in the eternal welcome that Heaven offers to all as One.

There is a place in you where this whole world has
been forgotten; where no memory of sin and of
illusion lingers still. There is a place in you which
time has left, and echoes of eternity are heard. There
is a resting place so still no sound except a hymn to
Heaven rises up to gladden God the Father and God
the Son. Where Both abide are They remembered,
Both. And where They are is Heaven and is peace.

Chapter 29 V: 1 (1-5)

Despite all our illusions and our "sinful" dreams of a world cut off
from God, none of us has ever left the Beloved's eternal embrace. This
being true, we each have access to the quiet realm of Spirit at all times.
Form loosens its grip on our awareness and the whole weighty world
dissolves when we enter the stillness of eternity within. Nothing moves
this sacred stillness, and the things of time simply fall away in the calm
of eternal Being. Always at our core, tranquil and ever undisturbed,
our Identity remains united with our Source. Yet, all too often we
allow pain and confusion to rob us of our peace. At such times it
seems impossible that we could simply lay them aside and find blissful
comfort in our own Self. Yet this is God's gift to each of us, and it is
never withheld. After all, how could what we *are* be withheld from us?
The text continues with these moving words, proclaiming the living
truth that is forever true: "The changelessness of Heaven is in you, so
deep within that nothing in this world but passes by, unnoticed and
unseen. The still infinity of endless peace surrounds you gently in its
soft embrace, so strong and quiet, tranquil in the might of its Creator,
nothing can intrude upon the sacred Son of God within."

Come to this place of refuge, where you can be
yourself in peace. Not through destruction, not
through a breaking out, but merely by a quiet melting
in. For peace will join you there, simply because
you have been willing to let go the limits you have
placed upon love, and joined it where it is and where
it led you, in answer to its gentle call to be at peace.

Chapter 18 VI: 14 (5-7)

The voice of Christ, the Buddha-nature, the pure Atman (Self), calls to us from our own deepest depths, inviting us to be at peace. We won't find this peace, this place of stillness, through any strenuous or dramatic effort as some would teach and believe. Being Who you actually are is *not* an achievement after all. The quiet peace of Enlightenment is simply the only option left to you once you become willing to let go of the limiting notion that you are less than love.

There is no violence at all in this escape. The body is not
attacked, but simply properly perceived. It does not limit
you, merely because you would not have it so. You are
not really "lifted out" of it; it cannot contain you. You go
where you would be, gaining, not losing, a sense of Self.

Chapter 18 VI: 13 (1-5)

The blissful shores of eternity will not to be taken by storm. If our
attempt to see and abide in peace is not itself inherently peaceful, then
the attempt will undoubtedly be in vain. What began as a search for
peace can all too quickly become yet another source of stress; one more
goal oriented endeavor which even in its apparent move toward peace,
chases peace on down the block. This is the classic error of all kinds of
human activity, both secular and spiritual.

Instead of grasping for inner advancement, simply trust the ocean
of conscious Love that abides in you, that *is* you, and don't let prayer or
meditation become a burdensome task. The *Course* does not instruct us
to flee from our bodily situation, but rather to see clearly that it cannot,
and need not, limit our awareness. The true nature of every so-called
one of us is eternal and infinite. The one Self that we *are* abides in peace,
forever at home in the Placeless Pavilion of God's endless Love.

The miracle comes quietly into the mind that stops
an instant and is still. It reaches gently from that quiet
time, and from the mind it healed in quiet then, to
other minds to share its quietness. And they will join
in doing nothing to prevent its radiant extension
back into the Mind which caused all minds to be.

Chapter 28 I: 11 (1-3)

The true miracle is simply reality dissolving illusion. It is the quiet healing of all madness. This gift can only be received in stillness, when our minds cease and desist for even a moment and we allow the truth to *be*. Yet this divine quiet is not merely some motionless state of immobility. The stillness of eternity extends its domain through welcome and joining, bringing all minds back to their original unity. There is no conquest or dominion in the extension of God's Kingdom, only a natural restoration to truth and the fullness of love.

A Miracle *is* justice. It is not a special gift to some,
to be withheld from others as less worthy, more
condemned, and thus apart from healing. Who
is there who can be separate from salvation, if its
purpose is the end of specialness? Where is salvation's
justice if some errors are unforgivable, and warrant
vengeance in place of healing and return of peace?

Chapter 25 IX: 6 (6-9)

The blessing of God that flows to us, and through us, is not kept in a little bottle, to be uncorked and distributed among the "worthy" ones. The notion that *anyone* deserves less than the full healing tide of God's infinite Love is the very hallmark of the ego's dark and twisted thought system. This is the cornerstone of separation; the doctrine of the damned.

God's Will is Oneness, which is (by definition) the same for each and all. Therefore, justice requires that no one receive vengeance as the reward for his or her mistakes. In the miracle of salvation, no one will be left behind. Even so, all errors are slated for correction; every shadow destined for the light. The whole world of differences and the imaginary life of specialness are only constructed and maintained on the basis of our forgetfulness of God. The peaceful healing of everything that the separation has tricked us into believing is salvation's sacred and singular purpose.

The only way to heal is to be healed. The miracle
extends without your help, but you are needed
that it can begin. Accept the miracle of healing,
and it will go forth because of what it is. It is its
nature to extend itself the instant it is born. And
it is born the instant it is offered and received.

Chapter 27 V: 1 (1-5)

Healing is the restoration of wholeness. Therefore, it cannot extend or
be offered from a state of unyielding separateness, wherein wholeness
has been lost sight of. Healing is the only true gift we can receive and
the only one of any real value we can offer one another. Just as light,
by its very nature, extends itself, the miracle of healing is radiant. The
moment you receive it, it goes forth, spreading out from its infinite and
timeless point of origin within you, to remove the suffering that the
separation has produced.

You understand that you are healed when you give
healing. You accept forgiveness as accomplished
in yourself when you forgive. You recognize your
brother as yourself, and thus do you perceive
that you are whole. There is no miracle you
cannot give, for all are given you. Receive them
now by opening the storehouse of your mind
where they are laid, and giving them away.

Workbook Lesson 159: 2 (1-5)

When we accept the healing force of God's Presence it becomes instantly clear that it was there all along. However it is only in "giving it away" that we come to truly understand what we have received. By simple virtue of Who we really Are, all of us have already received the full measure of God's boundless totality. Being His one Son, there is no miracle that has not been given to us, and not one that we are prevented from freely giving. In our oneness there is no room for holding anything apart. We *can* be healed and we can give healing to one another; we *can* offer and receive forgiveness. To do less, which has been our "go-to plan" for ages now, is to deny reality in favor of illusion. Yet if we so choose, we can leave all of that in the past, which was nothing but a bad dream, and in joyful celebration of our wholeness, begin to share the gracious gifts of healing and forgiveness.

Forget not that the healing of God's Son is
all the world is for. That is the only purpose
the Holy Spirit sees in it, and thus the only
one it has. Until you see the healing of the
Son as all you wish to be accomplished by
the world, by time and all appearances, you
will not know the Father nor yourself.

Chapter 24 VI: 4 (1-3)

If this sounds pretty much like an ultimatum to you, that's because it is. However, unlike the ultimatums we have become all too familiar with, this one is based on absolute and uncompromising Love. We are misled and misguided at every turn as we wander through this scratch-and-sniff universe. At one time a particular aspect of the world is our focus, and at another time we are completely captivated by some other facet of this dream world. To an extent this is natural; an ordinary function of finding yourself in a physical and seemingly limited dimension. Yet there *is* a single underlying principle here; a purpose and a meaning that dissolves all differences and brings every aspect of our varied experience into unity. The healing of God's Son is that single purpose. The separation, this brutal insistence that we are *not* one, has left us battered, broken, and alone. The certain and happy alternative to all of this is to see and accept God's healing Presence as the only truth in a world of illusion. I am reminded of a brief entry found among my travel notes from some years ago:

*Earth is just one more oozing outpost in Camp Grooviness
and as conscious beings we can either get with the
Program or live with the consequences.*

The Program is Infinite Love.

Each day, each hour and minute, even each second,
you are deciding between the crucifixion and
the resurrection; between the ego and the Holy
Spirit. The ego is the choice for guilt; the Holy
Spirit the choice for guiltlessness. The power of
decision is all that is yours. What you can decide
between is fixed, because there are no alternatives
except truth and illusion. And there is no overlap
between them, because they are opposites which
cannot be reconciled and cannot both be true.

Chapter 14 III: 4 (1-5)

The age-old question, "What is reality?" is the only pertinent question we can ask. How we answer that, determines our perception and our experience of absolutely everything else. The universe at large is either seen as a theater of fierce competition and mortal conflict or as a staging area for absolute Love and forgiveness. The choice is ours. One question: two possible answers. You see, the universe isn't really "at large" at all. It's a projection of our mind. From the ego's point of view this world is a hell-hole and somebody's got to pay. All the pain and heartless cruelty evident in the world is its proof that guilt rests somewhere, and calls for punishment if it is to be dealt with justly. The Holy Spirit's verdict is guiltlessness; the joyous resurrection of God's eternal Son to the perfection that he never really lost. The ego drives nails of condemnation into the flesh of God's innocent Son, whom it has sentenced to death. The Holy Spirit would bestow healing and comfort, seeing beyond all guilt, all illusion, to the light of truth that stands radiant and pure, as God created it.

Several paragraphs further in the text, we have this wonderful declaration: "Nothing can shake God's conviction of the perfect purity of everything that He created, for it *is* wholly pure. Do not decide against it, for being of Him it must be true. Peace abides in every mind that quietly accepts the plan God sets for its Atonement, relinquishing its own. You know not of salvation, for you do not understand it. Make no decisions about what it is or where it lies, but ask the Holy Spirit everything, and leave all decisions to His gentle counsel."

The power set in you in whom the Holy Spirit's
goal has been established is so far beyond your little
conception of the infinite that you have no idea how
great the strength that goes with you. And you can
use *this* in perfect safety. Yet for all its might, so great
it reaches past the stars and to the universe that lies
beyond them, your little faithlessness can make it
useless, if you would use the faithlessness instead.

Chapter 17 VII: 7 (1-3)

It seems that it's become fashionable of late to simply accept our powerlessness in the face of existence. We've come to see the whole "dust-in-the-wind, we are so small and meaningless" scenario as being a statement of real wisdom. In fairness, there is actually a grain of truth in this view because the ego *is* small, fleeting and futile in nature, and our bodies are just fancy dust- balls. But to stop there would be a colossal blunder, because we are not merely egos and bodies. Our nature as created by (and shared with), God, reflects the very infinity of Being, including but far outstretching the reaches of the universe itself. All the power of the Almighty; the full wattage of God, is there for use in bridging our perceived divisions, healing our sicknesses, and restoring us to sanity. Through failing to acknowledge the glorious truth, we continually sell ourselves short, and in so doing we sell each other down the river!

The boundless blessings of faith and the joy of eternity itself can be kept away only by our feeble faithlessness; so weak, yet the sole barricade against the blissful torrent of Heaven's grace. This world insists that the ego's evidence is more convincing than even truth itself. The Holy Spirit's goal, which is to make clear the guiltlessness of God's Son, is entirely unacceptable to our ego and its world. Interestingly, spell-check regards "guiltlessness" and "sinlessness," as well as "changelessness," to be non-existent words, while "faithlessness," which no doubt seems a great deal more plausible than these other states, enjoys a secure place in our vocabulary.

O my child, if you knew what God wills for you,
your joy would be complete! And what He wills has
happened, for it was always true. When the light
comes and you have said, "God's Will is mine," you
will see such beauty that you will know it is not of
you. Out of your joy you will create beauty in His
Name, for your joy could no more be contained
than His. The bleak little world will vanish into
nothingness, and your heart will be so filled with joy
that it will leap into Heaven, and into the Presence
of God. I cannot tell you what this will be like,
for your heart is not ready. Yet I can tell you, and
remind you often, that what God wills for Himself
He wills for you, and what He wills for you is yours.

Chapter 11 III: 3 (1-7)

We chronically seek for a little happiness, a tiny taste of joy. Yet if we could only see it, we would find we are awash in joy. The fathomless joy of God's infinite Being is all there is. This is the truth, beyond or other than which, there is nothingness. We are free even now, in this world of apparent limitation, to share Heaven's joy, unleashing the vision of beauty which alone can truly satisfy our hearts and unite us in the Oneness that has always been the truth. Our situation would be comical if it weren't for the needless, fully realistic, high-definition suffering it generates. On the same page as the above quotation, the *Course* paints a vivid portrait of our dilemma: "The Son of God is in need of comfort, for he knows not what he does, believing his will is not his own. The Kingdom is his, and yet he wanders homeless. At home in God he is lonely, and amid all his brothers his is friendless." This is not what God has willed and therefore it has never been true. To realize this is happiness itself; the great Good News that the limitless joy of God is the only and eternal reality.

All fear is past, because its source is gone, and all
its thoughts gone with it. Love remains the only
present state, whose Source is here forever and
forever. Can the world seem bright and clear and
safe and welcoming, with all my past mistakes
oppressing it, and showing me distorted forms of
fear? Yet in the present love is obvious, and its effects
apparent. All the world shines in reflection of its
holy light, and I perceive a world forgiven at last.

Workbook Lesson 293 1 (1-5)

Fear is the dark and heavy cloak that each of us uses to cover reality, weighing it down in our awareness and obscuring its true form from our sight. Yet fear only finds a refuge in thoughts that remain locked in place, bound by the countless deeds and misdeeds of the past. Fear is the past infiltrating and falsely assessing the present.

Love, being the very form of Formless Reality, is completely untouched by the past and wholly free of the distortions that twist our perception into a thousand fearful shapes. Love exists in the stillness of eternity, pouring forth without ceasing; a fount whose Source is always present, forever *now*. When we no longer wrap the world in fear, interpreting it in the context of a scandalous and threatening past, our vision is restored, and the beauty of the real world, the forgiven world, arises to our sight.

Every loving thought that the Son of God ever had
is eternal. The loving thoughts his mind perceives in
this world are the world's only reality. They are still
perceptions, because he still believes that he is separate.
Yet they are eternal because they are loving. And being
loving they are like the Father, and therefore cannot
die. The real world can actually be perceived. All that
is necessary is a willingness to perceive nothing else.

Chapter 11 VII: 2 (1-7)

In the grocery business they have a term for all the items that rot and go bad really quickly. They call them "perishables." On one level this world is like an aging sack of groceries; a collection of perishables, fast losing their savory quality and well on the way to becoming garbage. This is true of everything in the world of form. Not only the stuff of matter, but all of our perishable mental and emotional states as well. It's all shifting and changing, slipping through our fingers and no amount of clinging or denial can alter or slow the process. The only exception to this law of perishability is the loving thoughts we have in this world. Amid all the things in our awareness (hoarded, collected, neatly stacked or strewn about) only our loving thoughts bear the mark of eternity. Our Father, the Eternal One, *is* Love and the Source of it. Therefore our loving thoughts share His eternal nature. Love can never perish, even when everything around it crumbles and dissolves into vapor and dust. The real world is *this* world seen anew, with the light of Heaven upon it. This vision, this holy perception, is ours when we no longer seek a lesser form of sight, and we refuse to believe the pathetic version of the world revealed to unloving eyes.

Through the eyes of Christ, only the real world
exists and only the real world can be seen.
As you decide so will you see. And all that
you see but witnesses to your decision.

Chapter 12 VII: 11 (7-9)

Only Christ's vision of Oneness is real seeing, and it is only the world blessed by love and forgiveness that truly *exists*. So the question that begs an answer is, "Why all this other crap?" What is it that brought us to this illusory world of strife and deprivation? Here's a fun little quiz you can take at home: Can you say that you offer only love in response to any and every person or situation? Is attack an alien concept in your way of meeting the world? Do you look past all illusory and "sinful" appearances, judging others only as brothers and sisters in Christ, sharing equally with you in the inheritance of God's endless Blessing? If you answered "no" to any of these questions, and of course you did, there's your answer. We're seeing what we have decided to look upon. This assessment is a bit unnerving to say the least, but we are not left here to stumble on in the dark. A little earlier in Chapter 12 we find this inspiring passage. "Correction is for all who cannot see. To open the eyes of the blind is the Holy Spirit's mission, for He knows that they have not lost their vision, but merely sleep. He would awaken them from the sleep of forgetting to the remembering of God. Christ's eyes are open, and He will look upon whatever you see with love if you accept His vision as yours. The Holy Spirit keeps the vision of Christ for every Son of God who sleeps. In His sight the Son of God is perfect, and He longs to share His vision with you. He will show you the real world because God gave you Heaven."

What is one cannot be perceived as separate, and
the denial of the separation is the reinstatement of
knowledge. At the altar of God, the holy perception
of God's Son becomes so enlightened that light
streams into it, and the spirit of God's Son shines
in the Mind of the Father and becomes one with it.
Very gently does God shine upon Himself, loving
the extension of Himself that is His Son. The
world has no purpose as it blends into the purpose
of God. For the real world has slipped quietly into
Heaven, where everything eternal in it has always
been. There the Redeemer and the redeemed join
in perfect love of God and of each other. Heaven is
your home, and being in God it must also be in you.

Chapter 12 VI: 7 (1-7)

The whole of our experience has been a search for fulfillment. We've tried it all, to no avail. We have sought through all the means of separation, for that which only Unity can bestow. When we allow our perception to shift, receiving the timeless vision of Oneness, all of our seeking comes to an end. The treasure that seemed to endlessly elude us has in truth been present all along, there at the sacred altar within. In this knowledge and in this Love, every form of ignorance is undone at last. This is the one supreme experience that overwhelms every other perception, joyously replacing every lesser thought. We are pervaded by the eternal light of God, and in openness to the radiance of His endless Love, we find what was never really lost. Our union with the Father, and with one another in Him, is the lesson we've tried so hard and for so long *not* to learn. Yet this was the world's only reason for being; that what we offered it could be reflected to us until such time as we abandon all reflections in favor of Heaven's greater light.

This weary world, once such a torment, is at last forgiven and then finally absorbed into the formless heart of God. First we see the real world, then, no world, as the inexhaustible light of Heaven replaces all perception with true knowledge. "And then everything you made will be forgotten; the good and the bad, the false and the true. For as Heaven and earth become one, even the real world will vanish from your sight. The end of the world is not its destruction, but its translation into Heaven. The reinterpretation of the world is the transfer of all perception to knowledge." Chapter 11 VIII: 1 (6-9)

Would you learn how perfect and immaculate is the
holy altar on which your Father has placed Himself?
This you will recognize in the holy instant, in which
you willingly and gladly give over every plan but
His. For there lies peace, perfectly clear because
you have been willing to meet its conditions.

Chapter 15 IV: 4 (1-3)

How could it be that the Lord God has established His holy altar within
us when we so obviously lack the divine purity and sanctity that His
presence demands? Why would the Heavenly Father pitch His tent on
such homely soil? The truth is that the sacred site wherein He dwells is
the only part of us that has reality at all. Outside this holy "place" there
is nothing. Outside of truth there is only illusion. In the holy instant,
where all of our "hopeful" fantasies and fearful dreams do not exist, we
find that all of life is His pristine dwelling place. The peace of God's
Presence stands obvious when we let go of our schemes, our limited
opinions, and all of our requirements that life appear in some form that
we've sanctioned.

Each instant is a clean, untarnished birth, in
which the Son of God emerges from the past into
the present. And the present extends forever. It
is so beautiful and so clean and free of guilt that
nothing but happiness is there. No darkness is
remembered, and immortality and joy are now.

Chapter 15 I: 8 (4-7)

We spill forth from the heart of God, fresh and newly born in each
and every moment of our existence. The past does not cling to us, but
rather, it is *we* who do the clinging. In so doing, we color our present
awareness with all the ghostly hues of a shadowy and dismal past. Yet
even so, the light of truth shines forever undiminished. Reality has no
darkened nooks, and the boundless happiness of God is the only and
eternal truth of every instant.

In the holy instant nothing happens that has not
always been. Only the veil that has been drawn
across reality is lifted. Nothing has changed.
Yet the awareness of changelessness comes
swiftly as the veil of time is pushed aside.

Chapter 15 VI: 6 (1-4)

There has never been a time in which we were *not* one with God. Yet in our lack of vision, reality has remained unseen. We have constructed a veil of forgetfulness, tightly woven with threads we've gathered from the past, allowing this veil to completely hide the truth from our eyes. The moment we become willing to let the veil drop, the holy instant is revealed to us, and in that instant eternity is reclaimed as the glorious treasure that was never truly lost.

> A dream of judgment came into the mind that
> God created perfect as Himself. And in that
> dream was Heaven changed to hell, and God
> made enemy unto His Son. How can God's Son
> awaken from the dream? It is a dream of judgment.
> So must he judge not, and he will waken.

Chapter 29 IX: 2 (1-5)

Here is the Grand Scheme; the whole metaphysical enchilada, spelled out all nice and simple. Frequently however, the *practice* of non-judgment is nowhere near as neat and tidy as is the doctrine of non-judgment. We are the victims of a compulsion, a chronic behavior. Therefore, we often find ourselves knee deep in one conflict or another before it even occurs to us that, as Helen and Bill discovered, there *is* another way. We essentially pass judgment on every sound and sensation, every person or circumstance that crosses the threshold of our awareness. Our petty, baseless, and broad sweeping judgments have left us in a deep stupor; a sleep state plagued by nightmares of guilt and damnation. Yet our true Self, the Son of God, has no need of meaningless judgments and tormenting dreams of separation. We must begin to prefer Christ's vision to our own, and accept His vision *as* our own. Then there will be joy beyond measure, as we awaken in Oneness to find that sleep itself was only a dream.

You are as God created you. All else but this one
thing is folly to believe. In this one thought is
everyone set free. In this one truth are all illusions
gone. In this one fact is sinlessness proclaimed to
be forever part of everything, the central core of
its existence and its guarantee of immortality.

Workbook Lesson 191: 4 (2-6)

Nothing has ever happened that had the power to alter what you are.
However, plenty has occurred that had power to obstruct your sight,
making the truth seem nonexistent. All of that was foolishness; a mere
"game you play in which Identity can be denied." At our core, we all
share the one eternal and sinless Identity we were given in our creation.
This is the truth of us, the unassailable and *only* fact. You are as God
created you. This one thought is the open doorway to freedom and
to the immortal reality in which all illusions dissolve, having never
been.

Because reality is changeless is a miracle already there to
heal all things that change, and offer them to you to see
in happy form, devoid of fear. It will be given you to
look upon your brother thus. But not while you would
have it otherwise in some respects. For this but means
you would not have him healed and whole. The Christ
in him is perfect. Is it this that you would look upon?
Then let there be no dreams about him that you would
prefer to seeing this. And you will see the Christ in him
because you let Him come to you. And when He has
appeared to you, you will be certain you are like Him,
for He is the changeless in your brother and in you.

Chapter 30 VIII: 5 (1-9)

As long as we set our sights on a degraded version of the world and of
our brothers and sisters, we will find no shortage of evidence to support
our view. In this common world of objects and bodies we see only the
temporary, fleeting form of things, never resting our gaze on the thing
itself. There is a glorious perfection, eternal and as yet unseen, that remains
hidden behind the veil of mutability and mistrust. Yet all our fearful
dreams will continue to haunt us until such time as we choose the state of
wakefulness instead. The healing of all pain and the correction of every
error is already in place, awaiting only our acknowledgment that it may
become manifest and clear for all to see. The Christ in us is our only reality,
and His changeless Love will be all we *can see* the instant that it becomes
all we *want to see.* Chapter 24 spells it out like this: "Your brother's holiness
is sacrament and benediction unto you. His errors cannot withhold God's
blessing from himself, nor you who see him truly. His mistakes can cause
delay, which it is given you to take from him, that both may end a journey
that has never begun, and needs no end. What never was is not a part of
you. Yet you will think it is, until you realize that it is not a part of him
who stands beside you. He is the mirror of yourself, wherein you see the
judgment you have laid on both of you. The Christ in you beholds his
holiness. Your specialness looks on his body and beholds him not."

Not one light in Heaven but goes with you. Not
one Ray that shines forever in the Mind of God
but shines on you. Heaven is joined with you in
your advance to Heaven. When such great lights
have joined with you to give the little spark of your
desire the power of God Himself, can you remain in
darkness? You and your brother are coming home
together, after a long and meaningless journey that
you undertook apart, and that led nowhere. You have
found your brother, and you will light each other's
way. And from this light will the Great Rays extend
back into darkness and forward unto God, to shine
away the past and so make room for His eternal
Presence, in which everything is radiant in the light.

Chapter 18 III: 8 (1-7)

We are not, and never have been, deprived of God's infinite grace.
Forged in His original light, we live even now in the shadowless glow
of His Presence. No one can fail to reach Heaven, because no one ever
really left. We embarked on a mindless walkabout; a pilgrimage to
nowhere, intent on the notion that we were separate from our Source
and from each other. That can all be forgotten now, as we unite in the
sacred purpose of Heaven, moving on together toward the home we
never left.

The unalterable light of God is the framework on which everything
else rests. Ultimately the shining of His limitless light reveals that there
is no such thing as "everything else," all things being radiant; unified in
the One Presence that is His eternal Being. Although your run of the
mill physicist might disagree, this Non-dual wisdom is the long sought-
for "Theory of Everything." The Oneness of God's endless light is the
truth that subsumes all other facts and features into a sublime totality,
accounting for everything and negating nothing.

Forgive yourself your madness, and forget all
senseless journeys and all goal-less aims. They
have no meaning. You can not escape from what
you are. For God is merciful, and did not let His
Son abandon Him. For what He is be thankful,
for in that is your escape from madness and from
death. Nowhere but where He is can you be found.
There *is* no path that does not lead to Him.

Chapter 31 IV: 11 (1-7)

We've been the ones writing the script to this tragedy, which explains
why the plot has become so complicated and so cruel. Fortunately, the
roles we assigned to ourselves and others, as well as the objectives we
set, were never agreed upon by the Director. Therefore we have been
allowed to act out our dramas of guilt and betrayal, even unto death,
without them ever becoming the true story. Our escape from all this
madness lies in God's endless mercy. Salvation is ours because through
all of our nonsense, despite all our missteps and our thoughtlessness,
God never believed a word of it. He did not let us abandon Him. Our
wanderings away from truth have had no more meaning than the
journeys a dreamer takes at night, with his head resting there on the
pillow. Such journeys do not change the dreamer's location in the least.
And every dream, no matter how adventurous or spine-tingling, how
deadly or dangerous, merely leads him to the moment of awakening,
when the clear morning light forever replaces the world of slumber.

And so today we do not choose the way in which we
go to Him. But we do choose to let Him come. And
with this choice we rest. And in our quiet hearts and
open minds, His Love will blaze its pathway of itself.
What has not been denied is surely there, if it be true
and can be surely reached. God knows His Son, and
knows the way to him. He does not need His Son
to show Him how to find His way. Through every
opened door His Love shines outward from its home
within, and lightens up the world in innocence.

Workbook Lesson 189: 9 (1-8)

It seems a pretty sure bet that we'd end up lost rather than in Paradise,
were it left up to us to find the road to God, mapping out the path to
enlightenment as we saw fit. Fortunately this is not, and never has been
our task. It *is* required however, that we make the choice to let Him
come. The One who knows us, top to bottom, inside and out, not only
knows His way to us, but has no actual need of a "way," being already
fully Present within us. It is merely our own defenses that have kept
salvation at bay, denying reality, holding off the inevitable reunion with
our ever-present and Transcendent Source. There never has been any
reluctance on God's part. In this same Workbook Lesson we are told,
"Your part is simply to allow all obstacles you have interposed between
the Son and God the Father to be quietly removed forever." As we
abandon the myth of separation, our once troubled hearts and minds
are gathered up into His quiet embrace. We fling open the shutters of
our awareness only to find we are not so much letting His pure and
transforming light "in," as we are allowing it to shine "outward" from
its home within us, Where His Love has never ceased to shine.

Forgiveness

The unforgiving mind is full of fear, and offers love no room to be itself; no place where it can spread its wings in peace and soar above the turmoil of the world. The unforgiving mind is sad, without the hope of respite and release from pain. It suffers and abides in misery, peering about in darkness, seeing not, yet certain of the danger lurking there.

Workbook Lesson 121: 2 (1-3)

The unforgiving mind sees no mistakes, but only sins. It looks upon the world with sightless eyes, and shrieks as it beholds its own projections rising to attack its miserable parody of life. It wants to live, yet wishes it were dead. It wants forgiveness, yet it sees no hope. It wants escape, yet can conceive of none because it sees the sinful everywhere.

Workbook Lesson 121: 4 (1-5)

Forgiveness is acquired. It is not inherent in the mind, which cannot sin. As sin is an idea you taught yourself, forgiveness must be learned by you as well, but from a Teacher other than yourself, Who represents the other Self in you. Through Him you learn how to forgive the self you think you made, and let it disappear. Thus you return your mind as one to Him Who is your Self, and Who can never sin.

Workbook Lesson 121: 6 (1-5)

Each unforgiving mind presents you with an opportunity to teach your own how to forgive itself. Each one awaits release from hell through you, and turns to you imploringly for Heaven here and now. It has no hope, but you become its hope. And as its hope, do you become your own. The unforgiving mind must learn through your forgiveness that it has been saved from hell. And as you teach salvation, you will learn. Yet all your teaching and your learning will be not of you, but of the Teacher Who was given you to show the way to you.

Workbook Lesson 121: 7 (1-7)

It is sin's unreality that makes forgiveness natural and wholly sane, a deep relief to those who offer it; a quiet blessing where it is received. It does not countenance illusions, but collects them lightly, with a little laugh, and gently lays them at the feet of truth. And there they disappear entirely.

Workbook Lesson 134: 6 (1-3)

Forgiveness is the only thing that stands for truth in the illusions of the world. It sees their nothingness, and looks straight through the thousand forms in which they may appear. It looks on lies, but it is not deceived. It does not heed the self-accusing shrieks of sinners mad with guilt. It looks on them with quiet eyes, and merely says to them, "My brother, what you think is not the truth."

Workbook Lesson 134: 7 (1-5)

Christ's vision is the holy ground in which the lilies of forgiveness set their roots. This is their home. They can be brought from here back to the world, but they can never grow in its un-nourishing and shallow soil. They need the light and warmth and kindly care Christ's charity provides. They need the love with which He looks on them. And they become His messengers, who give as they received.

Workbook Lesson 159: 8 (1-6)

Take from His storehouse, that its treasures may increase. His lilies do not leave their home when they are carried back into the world. Their roots remain. They no not leave their source, but carry its beneficence with them, and turn the world into a garden like the one they came from, and to which they go again with added fragrance. Now they are twice blessed. The messages they brought from Christ have been delivered, and returned to them. And they return them gladly unto Him.

Workbook Lesson 159: 9 (1-7)

Behold the store of miracles set out for you to give. Are you not worthy of the gift, when God appointed it be given you? Judge not God's Son, but follow in the way He has established. Christ has dreamed the dream of a forgiven world. It is His gift, whereby a sweet transition can be made from death to life; from hopelessness to hope. Let us an instant dream with Him. His dream awakens us to truth. His vision gives the means for a return to our unlost and everlasting sanctity in God.

Workbook Lesson 159: 10 (1-8)

Now we are blessed, and now we bless the world. What we have looked upon we would extend, for we would see it everywhere. We would behold it shining with the grace of God in everyone. We would not have it be withheld from anything we look upon. And to ensure this holy sight is ours, we offer it to everything we see.

Workbook Lesson 187: 11 (1–5)

What can it be but arrogance to think your little errors cannot be undone by Heaven's justice? And what could this mean except that they are sins and not mistakes, forever uncorrectable, and to be met with vengeance, not with justice? Are you willing to be released from all effects of sin? You cannot answer this until you see all that the answer must entail. For if you answer "yes" it means you will forgo all values of this world in favor of the peace of Heaven. Not one sin would you retain. And not one doubt that this is possible will you hold dear that sin be kept in place. You mean that truth has greater value now than all illusions. And you recognize that truth must be revealed to you, because you know not what it is.

Chapter 25 IX: 1 (1–9)

Forgiveness is this world's equivalent of Heaven's justice. It translates the world of sin into a simple world, where justice can be reflected from beyond the gate behind which total lack of limits lies. Nothing in boundless love could need forgiveness. And what is charity within the world gives way to simple justice past the gate that opens into Heaven. No one forgives unless he has believed in sin, and still believes that he has much to be forgiven. Forgiveness thus becomes the means by which he learns he has done nothing to forgive. Forgiveness always rests upon the one who offers it, until he sees himself as needing it no more. And thus is he returned to his real function of creating, which his forgiveness offers him again.

Chapter 26 IV: 1 (1–7)

Forgiveness turns the world of sin into a world of glory, wonderful to see. Each flower shines in light, and every bird sings of the joy of Heaven. There is no sadness and there is no parting here, for everything is totally forgiven. And what has been forgiven must join, for nothing stands between to keep them separate and apart. The sinless must perceive that they are one, for nothing stands between to push the other off. And in the space that sin left vacant do they join as one, in gladness recognizing what is part of them has not been kept apart and separate.

Chapter 26 IV: 2 (1-6)

The holy place on which you stand is but the space that sin has left. And here you see the face of Christ, arising in its place. Who could behold the face of Christ and not recall His Father as He really is? Who could fear love, and stand upon the ground where sin has left a place for Heaven's altar to rise and tower far above the world, and reach beyond the universe to touch the Heart of all creation? What is Heaven but a song of gratitude and love and praise by everything created to the Source of its creation? The holiest of altars is set where once sin was believed to be. And here does every light of Heaven come, to be rekindled and increased in joy. For here is what was lost restored to them, and all their radiance made whole again.

Chapter 26 IV: 3 (1-8)

Forgiveness brings no little miracles to lay before the gate of Heaven. Here the Son of God Himself comes to receive each gift that brings him nearer to his home. Not one is lost, and none is cherished more than any other. Each reminds him of his Father's Love as surely as the rest. And each one teaches him that what he feared he loves the most. What but a miracle could change his mind, so that he understands that love cannot be feared? What other miracle is there but this? And what else need there be to make the space between you disappear?

Chapter 26 IV: 4 (1-8)

Where sin once was perceived will rise a world that will become an altar to the truth, and you will join the lights of Heaven there, and sing their song of gratitude and praise. And as they come to you to be complete, so will you go with them. For no one hears the song of Heaven and remains without a voice that adds its power to the song, and makes it sweeter still. And each one joins the singing at the altar that was raised within the tiny spot that sin proclaimed to be its own. And what was tiny then has soared into a magnitude of song in which the universe has joined with but a single voice.

Chapter 26 IV: 5 (1-5)

This tiny spot of sin that stands between you and your brother still is holding back the happy opening of Heaven's gate. How little is the hindrance that withholds the wealth of Heaven from you. And how great will be the joy in Heaven when you join the mighty chorus to the Love of God!

Chapter 26 IV: 6 (1-3)

You who believe there is a little gap between you and your brother, do not see that it is here you are as prisoners in a world perceived to be existing here. The world you see does not exist, because the place where you perceive it is not real. The gap is carefully concealed in fog, and misty pictures rise to cover it with vague uncertain forms and changing shapes, forever unsubstantial an unsure. Yet in the gap is nothing. And there are no awesome secrets and no darkened tombs where terror rises from the bones of death. Look at the little gap, and you behold the innocence and emptiness of sin that you will see within yourself, when you have lost the fear of recognizing love.

Chapter 28 V: 7 (1-6)

From the forgiven world the Son of God is lifted easily into his home. And there he knows that he has always rested there in peace. Even salvation will become a dream, and vanish from his mind. For salvation is the end of dreams, and with the closing of the dream will have no meaning. Who, awake in Heaven, could dream that there could ever be need of salvation?

Chapter 17 II: 7 (1-5)

Guiltlessness

As you look upon yourself and judge what you do honestly, you may be temped to wonder how you can be guiltless. Yet consider this: You are not guiltless in time, but in eternity. You have "sinned" in the past, but there is no past. Always has no direction. Time seems to go in one direction, but when you reach its end it will roll up like a long carpet spread along the past behind you, and will disappear. As long as you believe the Son of God is guilty you will walk along this carpet, believing that it leads to death. And the journey will seem long and cruel and senseless, for so it is.

Chapter 13 I: 3 (1-7)

The journey the Son of God has set himself is useless indeed, but the journey on which his Father sets him is one of release and joy. The Father is not cruel, and His Son cannot hurt himself. The retaliation that he fears and that he sees will never touch him, for although he believes in it the Holy Spirit knows it is not true. The Holy Spirit stands at the end of time, where you must be because He is with you. He has already undone everything unworthy of the Son of God, for such was His mission, given Him by God. And what God gives has always been.

Chapter 13 I: 4 (1-6)

You will see me as you learn the Son of God is guiltless. He has always sought his guiltlessness, and he has found it. For everyone is seeking to escape from the prison he has made, and the way to find release is not denied him. Being in him, he has found it. *When* he finds it is only a matter of time, and time is but an illusion. For the Son of God is guiltless now, and the brightness of his purity shines untouched forever in God's Mind. God's Son will always be as he was created. Deny your world and judge him not, for his eternal guiltlessness is in the Mind of his Father, and protects him forever.

Chapter 13 I: 5 (1-8)

When you have accepted the Atonement for yourself, you will realize there is no guilt in God's Son. And only as you look upon him as guiltless can you understand his oneness. For the idea of guilt brings a belief in condemnation of one by another, projecting separation in place of unity. You can condemn only yourself, and by so doing you cannot know that you are God's Son. You have denied the condition of his being, which is his perfect blamelessness. Out of love he was created, and in love he abides. Goodness and mercy have always followed him, for he has always extended the Love of his Father.

Chapter 13 I: 6 (1- 7)

As you perceive the holy companions who travel with you, you will realize that there is no journey, but only an awakening. The Son of God, who sleepeth not, has kept faith with his Father for you. There is no road to travel on, and no time to travel through. For God waits not for His Son in time, being forever unwilling to be without him. And so it has always been. Let the holiness of God's Son shine away the cloud of guilt that darkens your mind, and by accepting his purity as yours, learn of him that it *is* yours.

Chapter 13 I: 7 (1-6)

Behold your brothers in their freedom, and learn of them how to be free of darkness. The light in you will waken them, and they will not leave you asleep. The vision of Christ is given the very instant that it is perceived. Where everything is clear, it is all holy. The quietness of its simplicity is so compelling that you will realize it is impossible to deny the simple truth. For there is nothing else. God is everywhere, and His Son is in Him with everything. Can he sing the dirge of sorrow when this is true?

Chapter 14 II: 8 (1-8)

Guilt makes you blind, for while you see one spot of guilt within you, you will not see the light. And by projecting it the world seems dark, and shrouded in your guilt. You throw a dark veil over it, and cannot see it because you cannot look within. You are afraid of what you would see there, but it is not there. *The thing you fear is gone.* If you would look within you would see only the Atonement, shining in quiet and in peace upon the altar to your Father.

Chapter 13 IX: 7 (1-6)

Do not be afraid to look within. The ego tells you all is black with guilt within you, and bids you not to look. Instead, it bids you look upon your brothers, and see the guilt in them. Yet this you cannot do without remaining blind. For those who see their brothers in the dark, and guilty in the dark in which they shroud them, are too afraid to look upon the light within. Within you is not what you believe is there, and what you put your faith in. Within you is the holy sign of perfect faith your Father has in you. He does not value you as you do. He knows Himself, and knows the truth in you. He knows there is no difference, for He knows not of differences. Can you see guilt where God knows there is perfect innocence? You can deny His knowledge, but you cannot change it. Look, then, upon the light He placed within you, and learn that what you feared was there has been replaced with love.

Chapter 13 IX: 8 (1-13)

The Holy Spirit cannot punish sin. Mistakes He recognizes, and would correct them all as God entrusted Him to do. But sin He knows not, nor can He recognize mistakes that cannot be corrected. For a mistake that cannot be corrected is meaningless to Him. Mistakes are *for* correction, and they call for nothing else. What calls for punishment must call for nothing. Every mistake *must* be a call for love.

Chapter 19 III: 4 (1-7)

Dream softly of your sinless brother, who unites with you in holy innocence. And from this dream the Lord of Heaven will Himself awaken His beloved Son. Dream of your brother's kindnesses instead of dwelling in your dreams on his mistakes. Select his thoughtfulness to dream about instead of counting up the hurts he gave. Forgive him his illusions, and give thanks to him for all the helpfulness he gave. And do not brush aside his many gifts because he is not perfect in your dreams.

Chapter 27 VII: 15 (1-6)

Decide that God is right and you are wrong about yourself. He created you out of Himself, but still within Him. He knows what you are. Remember that there is no second to Him. There cannot, therefore, be anyone without His Holiness, nor anyone unworthy of His perfect Love.

Chapter 14 IV: 4 (5-9)

Unless you are guiltless you cannot know God, Whose Will is that you know Him. Therefore, you *must* be guiltless. Yet if you do not accept the necessary conditions for knowing Him, you have denied Him and do not recognize Him, though He is all around you. He cannot be known without His Son, whose guiltlessness is the condition for knowing Him. Accepting His Son as guilty is denial of the Father so complete, that knowledge is swept away from recognition in the very mind where God Himself has placed it.

Chapter 14 IV: 7 (1-5)

When you seem to see some twisted form of the original error rising to frighten you, say only, "God is not fear, but Love," and it will disappear. The truth will save you. It has not left you, to go out into the mad world and so depart from you. Inward is sanity; insanity is outside you. You but believe it is the other way; that truth is outside, and error and guilt within.

Chapter 18 I: 7 (1-5)

Vision

My grievances show me what is not there, and hide from me what I would see. Recognizing this, what do I want my grievances for? They keep me in darkness and hide the light. Grievances and light cannot go together, but light and vision must be joined for me to see. To see, I must lay grievances aside. I want to see, and this will be the means by which I will succeed.

Workbook Lesson 85: 1 (2-7)

Idle wishes and grievances are partners or co-makers in picturing the world you see. The wishes of the ego gave rise to it, and the ego's need for grievances, which are necessary to maintain it, peoples it with figures that seem to attack you and call for "righteous" judgment. These figures become the middlemen the ego employs to traffic in grievances. They stand between your awareness and your brothers' reality. Beholding them, you do not know your brothers or your Self.

Workbook Lesson 73: 2 (1-5)

Your picture of the world can only mirror what is within. The source of neither light nor darkness can be found without. Grievances darken your mind, and you look out on a darkened world. Forgiveness lifts the darkness, reasserts your will, and lets you look upon a world of light.

Workbook Lesson 73: 5 (1-4)

Your purpose is to see the world through your own holiness. Thus are you and the world blessed together. No one loses; nothing is taken away from anyone; everyone gains through your holy vision. It signifies the end of sacrifice because it offers everyone his full due. And he is entitled to everything because it is his birthright as a Son of God.

Workbook Lesson 37: 1 (2-6)

Dwell not upon the past today. Keep a completely open mind, washed of all past ideas and clean of every concept you have made. You have forgiven the world today. You can look upon it now as if you never saw it before.

Workbook Lesson 75: 6 (1-4)

Realize that your forgiveness entitles you to vision. Understand that the Holy Spirit never fails to give the gift of sight to the forgiving. Believe He will not fail you now. You have forgiven the world. He will be with you as you watch and wait. He will show you what true vision sees. It is His Will, and you have joined with Him. Wait patiently for Him. He will be there. The light has come. You have forgiven the world.

Workbook Lesson 75: 7 (1-11)

Look deep within you, undismayed by all the little thoughts and foolish goals you pass as you ascend to meet the Christ in you.

He will be there. And you can reach Him now. What could you rather look upon in place of Him Who waits that you may look on Him? What little thought has power to hold you back? What foolish goal can keep you from success when He Who calls to you is God Himself?

Workbook Lesson 100: 8 (5), 9 (1-5)

Leave, then, your needs to Him. He will supply them with no emphasis at all upon them. What comes to you of Him comes safely, for He will ensure it never can become a dark spot, hidden in your mind and kept to hurt you. Under His guidance you will travel light and journey lightly, for His sight is ever on the journey's end, which is His goal. God's Son is not a traveler through outer worlds. However holy his perception may become, no world outside himself holds his inheritance. Within himself he has no needs, for light needs nothing but to shine in peace, and from itself to let the rays extend in quiet to infinity.

Whenever you are tempted to undertake a useless journey that would lead away from light, remember what you really want, and say:

The Holy Spirit leads me unto Christ, and where else would I go?

What need have I but to awake in Him?

Chapter 13 VII: 13 (1-7), 14 (1-2)

This is the miracle of creation; *that it is one forever.* Every miracle you offer to the Son of God is but the true perception of one aspect of the whole. Though every aspect *is* the whole, you cannot know this until you see that every aspect is the same, perceived in the same light and therefore one. Everyone seen without the past thus brings you nearer to the end of time by bringing healed and healing sight into the darkness, and enabling the world to see. For light must come into the darkened world to make Christ's vision possible even here. Help Him to give His gift of light to all who think they wander in the darkness, and let Him gather them into His quiet sight that makes them one.

Chapter 13 VIII: 5 (1-6)

You have no conception of the limits you have placed on your perception, and no idea of all the loveliness that you could see. But this you must remember; the attraction of guilt opposes the attraction of God. His attraction for you remains unlimited, but because your power, being His, is as great as His, you can turn away from love. What you invest in guilt you withdraw from God. And your sight grows weak and dim and limited, for you have attempted to separate the Father from the Son, and limit their communication. Seek not Atonement in further separation. And limit not your vision of God's Son to what interferes with his release, and what the Holy Spirit must undo to set him free. For his belief in limits *has* imprisoned him.

Chapter 15 IX: 6 (1-8)

Christ's vision is a miracle. It comes from far beyond itself, for it reflects eternal love and the rebirth of love which never dies, but has been kept obscure. Christ's vision pictures Heaven, for it sees a world so like to Heaven that what God created perfect can be mirrored there. The darkened glass the world presents can show but twisted images in broken parts. The real world pictures Heaven's innocence.

Workbook Lesson 159: 3 (1-5)

Christ's vision is the miracle in which all miracles are born. It is their source, remaining with each miracle you give, and yet remaining yours. It is the bond by which the giver and receiver are united in extension here on earth, as they are one in Heaven. Christ beholds no sin in anyone. And in His sight the sinless are as one. Their holiness was given by His Father and Himself.

Workbook Lesson 159: 4 (1-6)

Christ's vision is the bridge between the worlds. And in its power can you safely trust to carry you from this world into one made holy by forgiveness. Things which seem quite solid here are merely shadows there; transparent, faintly seen, at times forgotten, and never able to obscure the light that shines beyond them. Holiness has been restored to vision, and the blind can see.

Workbook Lesson 159: 5 (1-4)

God's Love

Be quiet in your faith in Him Who loves you, and would lead you out of insanity. Madness may be your choice, but not your reality. Never forget the Love of God, Who has remembered you. For it is quite impossible that He could ever let His Son drop from the loving Mind wherein he was created, and where his abode was fixed in perfect peace forever.

Chapter 14 III: 15 (5-8)

How gracious it is to decide all things through Him Whose equal Love is given equally to all alike! He leaves you no one outside you. And so He gives you what is yours, because your Father would have you share it with Him. In everything be led by Him, and do not reconsider. Trust Him to answer quickly, surely, and with Love for everyone who will be touched in any way by the decision. And everyone will be. Would you take unto yourself the sole responsibility for deciding what can bring only good to everyone? Would you know this?

Chapter 14 III: 17 (1-8)

Your Father has not denied you. He does not retaliate, but He does call to you to return. When you think He has not answered your call, you have not answered His. He calls to you from every part of the Sonship, because of His Love for His Son. If you hear His message He has answered you, and you will learn of Him if you hear aright. The Love of God is in everything He created, for His Son is everywhere. Look with peace upon your brothers, and God will come rushing into your heart in gratitude for your gift to Him.

Chapter 10 V: 7 (1-7)

Only the eternal can be loved, for love does not die. What is of God is His forever, and you are of God. Would He allow Himself to suffer? And would He offer His Son anything that is not acceptable to Him? If you will accept yourself as God created you, you will be incapable of suffering. Yet to do this you must acknowledge Him as your Creator. This is not because you will be punished otherwise. It is merely because your acknowledgment of your Father is the acknowledgment of yourself as you are. Your Father created you wholly without sin, wholly without pain and wholly without suffering of any kind. If you deny Him you bring sin, pain and suffering into your own mind because of the power He gave it. Your mind is capable of creating worlds, but it can also deny what it creates because it is free.

Chapter 10 V: 9 (1-11)

You do not realize how much you have denied yourself, and how much God, in His Love, would not have it so. Yet He would not interfere with you, because He would not know His Son if he were not free. To interfere with you would be to attack Himself, and God is not insane. When you deny Him *you* are insane. Would you have Him share your insanity? God will never cease to love His Son, and His Son will never cease to love Him. That was the condition of His Son's creation, fixed forever in the Mind of God. To know that is sanity. To deny it is insanity. God gave Himself to you in your creation, and His gifts are eternal. Would you deny yourself to Him?

Chapter 10 V: 10 (1-11)

It is God's Will that nothing touch His Son except Himself, and nothing else comes nigh unto him. He is as safe from pain as God Himself, Who watches over him in everything. The world about him shines with love because God placed him in Himself where pain is not, and love surrounds him without end or flaw. Disturbance of his peace can never be. In perfect sanity he looks on love, for it is all about him and within him. He must deny the world of pain the instant he perceives the arms of love around him. And from this point of safety he looks quietly about him and recognizes that the world is one with him.

Chapter 13 VII: 7 (1-7)

The world I see holds my fearful self-image in place, and guarantees its continuance. While I see the world as I see it now, truth cannot enter my awareness. I would let the door behind this world be opened for me, that I may look past it to the world that reflects the Love of God.

Workbook Lesson 56: 3 (2-4)

Behind every image I have made, the truth remains unchanged. Behind every veil I have drawn across the face of love, its light remains undimmed. Beyond all my insane wishes is my will, united with the Will of my Father. God is still everywhere and in everything forever. And we who are part of Him will yet look past all appearances, and recognize the truth beyond them all.

Workbook Lesson 56: 4 (2-6)

You are one Self, in perfect harmony with all there is, and all that there will be. You are one Self, the holy Son of God, united with your brothers in that Self; united with your Father in His Will. Feel this one Self in you, and let It shine away all your illusions and your doubts. This is your Self, the Son of God Himself, sinless as Its Creator, with His strength within you and His Love forever yours. You are one Self, and it is given you to feel this Self within you, and to cast all your illusions out of the one Mind that is this Self, the holy truth in you.

Workbook Lesson 95: 13 (1- 5)

Grace is acceptance of the Love of God within a world of seeming hate and fear. By grace alone the hate and fear are gone, for grace presents a state so opposite to everything the world contains, that those whose minds are lighted by the gift of grace can not believe the world of fear is real.

Workbook Lesson 169: 2 (1-2)

Because of your Father's Love you can never forget Him, for no one can forget what God Himself placed in his memory. You can deny it, but you cannot lose it. A voice will answer every question you ask, and a vision will correct the perception of everything you see. For what you have made invisible is the only truth, and what you have not heard is the only Answer. God would reunite you with yourself, and did not abandon you in your distress. You are waiting only for Him, and do not know it. Yet His memory shines in your mind and cannot be obliterated. It is no more past than future, being forever always.

Chapter 12 VIII: 4 (1-7)

In the temple, Holiness waits quietly for the return of them that love it. The Presence knows they will return to purity and to grace. The graciousness of God will take them gently in, and cover all their sense of pain and loss with the immortal assurance of their Father's Love. There, fear of death will be replaced with joy of life. For God is life, and they abide in life. Life is as holy as the Holiness by which it was created. The Presence of Holiness lives in everything that lives, for Holiness created life, and leaves not what It created holy as Itself.

Chapter 14 IX: 4 (1-7)

Love is not learned. Its meaning lies within itself. And learning ends when you have recognized all it is *not*. That is the interference; that is what needs to be undone. Love is not learned, because there never was a time in which you knew it not. Learning is useless in the Presence of your Creator, Whose acknowledgment of you and yours of Him so far transcend all learning that everything you learned is meaningless, replaced forever by the knowledge of love and its one meaning.

Chapter 18 IX: 12 (1-6)

Idols

A concept of the self is made by you. It bears no likeness to yourself at all. It is an idol, made to take the place of your reality as Son of God.

Chapter 31 V: 2 (1-3)

Seek not outside yourself. For it will fail, and you will weep each time an idol falls. Heaven cannot be found where it is not, and there can be no peace excepting there. Each idol that you worship when God calls will never answer in His place. There is no other answer you can substitute, and find the happiness His answer brings. Seek not outside yourself. For all your pain comes simply from a futile search for what you want, insisting where it must be found. What if it is not there? Do you prefer that you be right or happy? Be you glad that you are told where happiness abides, and seek no longer elsewhere. You will fail. But it is given you to know the truth, and not to seek for it outside yourself.

Chapter 29 VII: 1 (1-12)

All idols of this world were made to keep the truth within from being known to you, and to maintain allegiance to the dream that you must find what is outside yourself to be complete and happy. It is vain to worship idols in the hope of peace. God dwells within, and your completion lies in Him. No idol takes His place. Look not to idols. Do not seek outside yourself.

Chapter 29 VII: 6 (1-6)

God has not many Sons, but only One. Who can have more, and who be given less? In Heaven would the Son of God but laugh, if idols could intrude upon his peace.

Chapter 29 VIII: 9 (1-3)

An idol is an image of your brother that you would value more than what he is. Idols are made that he may be replaced, no matter what their form. And it is this that never is perceived and recognized. Be it a body or a thing, a place, a situation or a circumstance, an object owned or wanted, or a right demanded or achieved, it is the same.

Let not their form deceive you. Idols are but substitutes for your reality. In some way, you believe they will complete your little self, for safety in world perceived as dangerous, with forces massed against your confidence and peace of mind. They have the power to supply your lacks, and add the value that you do not have. No one believes in idols who has not enslaved himself to littleness and loss. And thus must seek beyond his little self for strength to raise his head, and stand apart from all the misery the world reflects. This is the penalty for looking not within for certainty and quiet calm that liberates you from the world, and lets you stand apart, in quiet and in peace.

Chapter 29 VIII: 1 (6-9), 2 (1-7)

This world of idols *is* a veil across the face of Christ, because its purpose is to separate your brother from yourself. A dark and fearful purpose, yet a thought without the power to change one blade of grass from something living to a sign of death.

Chapter 29 VIII: 4 (1-2)

The ego is idolatry; the sign of limited and separated self, born in a body, doomed to suffer and to end its life in death. It is the "will" that sees the Will of God as enemy, and takes a form in which it is denied. The ego is the "proof" that strength is weak and love is fearful, life is really death, and what opposes God alone is true.

Workbook: What Is the Ego? 1 (1-3)

Where is an idol? Nowhere! Can there be a gap in what is infinite, a place where time can interrupt eternity? A place of darkness set where all is light, a dismal alcove separated off from what is endless, *has* no place to be. An idol is beyond where God has set all things forever, and has left no room for anything to be except His Will. Nothing and nowhere must an idol be, while God is everything and everywhere.

Chapter 29 VIII: 7 (1-6)

The Holy Instant

How long can it take to be where God would have you be? For you are where you have forever been and will forever be. All that you have, you have forever. The blessed instant reaches out to encompass time, as God extends Himself to encompass you. You who have spent days, hours and even years in chaining your brothers to your ego in an attempt to support it and uphold its weakness, do not perceive the Source of strength. In this holy instant you will unchain all your brothers, and refuse to support either their weakness or your own.

Chapter 15 II: 3 (1-6)

Time is your friend, if you leave it to the Holy Spirit to use. He needs but very little to restore God's whole power to you. He Who transcends time for you understands what time is for. Holiness lies not in time, but in eternity. There never was an instant in which God's Son could lose his purity. His changeless state is beyond time, for his purity remains forever beyond attack and without variability. Time stands still in his holiness, and changes not. And so it is no longer time at all. For caught in the single instant of the eternal sanctity of God's creation, it is transformed into forever. Give the eternal instant, that eternity may be remembered for you, in that shining instant of perfect release. Offer the miracle of the holy instant through the Holy Spirit, and leave His giving it to you to Him.

Chapter 15 I: 15 (1-11)

I stand within the holy instant, as clear as you would have me. And the extent to which you learn to accept me is the measure of the time in which the holy instant will be yours. I call to you to make the holy instant yours at once, for the release from littleness in the mind of the host of God depends on willingness, and not on time.

Chapter 15 IV: 5 (1-3)

The reason this course is simple is that truth is simple. Complexity is of the ego, and is nothing more that the ego's attempt to obscure the obvious. You could live forever in the holy instant, beginning now and reaching to eternity, but for a very simple reason. Do not obscure the simplicity of this reason, for if you do, it will be only because you prefer not to recognize it and not to let it go. The simple reason, simply stated, is this: The holy instant is a time in which you receive and give perfect communication. This means, however, that it is a time in which your mind is open, both to receive and give. It is the recognition that all minds are in communication. It therefore seeks to change nothing, but merely to accept everything.

Chapter 15 IV: 6 (1-8)

As the ego would limit your perception of your brothers to the body, so would the Holy Spirit release your vision and let you see the Great Rays shining from them, so unlimited that they reach to God. It is this shift to vision that is accomplished in the holy instant. Yet it is needful for you to learn just what this shift entails, so you will become willing to make it permanent. Given this willingness it will not leave you, for it *is* permanent. Once you have accepted it as the only perception you want, it is translated into knowledge by the part that God Himself plays in the Atonement, for it is the only step in it He understands. Therefore, in this there will be no delay when you are ready for it. God is ready now, but you are not.

Chapter 15 IX: 1 (1-7)

The little breath of eternity that runs through time like golden light is all the same; nothing before it, nothing afterwards.

You look upon each holy instant as a different point in time. It never changes. All that it ever held or will ever hold is here right now. The past takes nothing from it, and the future will add no more. Here, then, is everything. Here is the loveliness of your relationship, with means and end in perfect harmony already. Here is the perfect faith that you will one day offer to your brother already offered you; and here the limitless forgiveness you will give him already given, the face of Christ you yet will look upon already seen.

Chapter 20 V: 5 (8), 6 (1-7)

The holy instant does not come from your little willingness alone. It is always the result of your small willingness combined with the unlimited power of God's Will. You have been wrong in thinking that it is needful to prepare yourself for Him. It is impossible to make arrogant preparations for holiness, and not believe that it is up to you to establish the conditions for peace. God has established them. They do not wait upon your willingness for what they are. Your willingness is needed only to make it possible to teach you what they are. If you maintain you are unworthy of learning this, you are interfering with the lesson by believing that you must make the learner different. You did not make the learner, nor can you make him different. Would you first make a miracle yourself, and then expect one to be made *for* you?

Chapter 18 IV: 4 (1-10)

There is no escape from fear in the ego's use of time. For time, according to its teaching, is nothing but a teaching device for compounding guilt until it becomes all-encompassing, demanding vengeance forever.

The Holy Spirit would undo all of this *now*. Fear is not of the present, but only of the past and future, which do not exist. There is no fear in the present when each instant stands clear and separated from the past, without its shadow reaching out into the future.

Chapter 15 I: 7 (6-7), 8 (1-3)

This lesson takes no time. For what is time without a past and future? It has taken time to misguide you so completely, but it takes no time at all to be what you are. Begin to practice the Holy Spirit's use of time as a teaching aid to happiness and peace. Take this very instant, now, and think of it as all there is of time. Nothing can reach you here out of the past, and it is here that you are completely absolved, completely free and wholly without condemnation. From this holy instant wherein holiness was born again you will go forth in time without fear, and with no sense of change with time.

Chapter 15 I: 9 (1-7)

Time is inconceivable without change, yet holiness does not change. Learn from this instant more than merely that hell does not exist. In this redeeming instant lies Heaven. And Heaven will not change, for the birth into the holy present is salvation from change. Change is an illusion, taught by those who cannot see themselves as guiltless. There is no change in Heaven because there is no change in God. In the holy instant, in which you see yourself as bright with freedom, you will remember God. For remembering Him *is* to remember freedom.

Chapter 15 I: 10 (1-8)

You will never give this holy instant to the Holy Spirit on behalf of your release while you are unwilling to give it to your brothers on behalf of theirs. For the instant of holiness is shared, and cannot be yours alone. Remember, then, when you are tempted to attack a brother, that his instant of release is yours. Miracles are the instants of release you offer, and will receive. They attest to your willingness to *be* released, and to offer time to the Holy Spirit for His use of it.

Chapter 15 I: 12 (1-5)

Our True Identity

One holy thought like this and you are free: You are the holy Son of God Himself. And with this holy thought you learn as well that you have freed the world. You have no need to use it cruelly, and then perceive this savage need in it. You set it free of your imprisonment. You will not see a devastating image of yourself walking the world in terror, with the world twisting in agony because your fears have laid the mark of death upon its heart.

Workbook Lesson 191: 6 (1-5)

You who perceive yourself as weak and frail, with futile hopes and devastating dreams, born to die, to weep and suffer pain, hear this: All power is given unto you in earth and Heaven. There is nothing that you cannot do. You play the game of death, of being helpless, pitifully tied to dissolution in a world which shows no mercy to you. Yet when you accord it mercy, will its mercy shine on you.

Workbook Lesson 191: 9 (1-4)

In the ultimate sense, reincarnation is impossible. There is no past or future, and the idea of birth into a body has no meaning either once or many times. Reincarnation cannot, then, be true in any real sense. Our only question should be, "Is the concept helpful?" And that depends, of course, on what it is used for. If it is used to strengthen the recognition of the eternal nature of life, it is helpful indeed. Is any other question about it really useful in lighting up the way? Like many other beliefs, it can be bitterly misused. At least, such misuse offers preoccupation and perhaps pride in the past. At worst, it induces inertia in the present. In between, many kinds of folly are possible.

Reincarnation would not, under any circumstances, be the problem to be dealt with *now*. If it were responsible for some of the difficulties the individual faces now, his task would still be only to escape from them now. If he is laying the groundwork for a future life, he can still work out his salvation only now. To some, there may be comfort in the concept, and if it heartens them its value is self-evident. It is certain, however, that the way to salvation can be found by those who believe in reincarnation and by those who do not. The idea cannot, therefore, be regarded as essential to the curriculum. There is always some risk in seeing the present in terms of the past. There is always some good in any thought which strengthens the idea that life and the body are not the same.

Manual For Teachers: Is Reincarnation So?

Then let the Son of God awaken from his sleep, and opening his holy eyes, return again to bless the world he made. In error it began, but it will end in the reflection of his holiness. And he will sleep no more and dream of death. Then join with me today. Your glory is the light that saves the world. Do not withhold salvation longer. Look about the world, and see the suffering there. Is not your heart willing to bring your weary brothers rest?

Workbook Lesson 191: 10 (1-8)

In stillness we will hear God's Voice today without intrusion of our petty thoughts, without our personal desires, and without all judgment of His holy Word. We will not judge ourselves today, for what we are can not be judged. We stand apart from all the judgments which the world has laid upon the Son of God. It knows him not. Today we will not listen to the world, but wait in silence for the Word of God.

Workbook Lesson 125: 3 (1-5)

He has not waited until you return your mind to Him to give His Word to you. He has not hid Himself from you, while you have wandered off a little while from Him. He does not cherish the illusions which you hold about yourself. He knows His Son, and wills that he remain as part of Him regardless of his dreams; regardless of his madness that his will is not his own.

Workbook Lesson 125: 5 (1-4)

It is your voice to which you listen as He speaks to you. It is your word He speaks. It is the Word of freedom and of peace, of unity of will and purpose, with no separation nor division in the single Mind of Father and of Son. In quiet listen to your Self today, and let Him tell you God has never left His Son, and you have never left your Self.

Workbook Lesson 125: 8 (1-4)

You are afraid of me because you looked within and are afraid of what you saw. Yet you could not have seen reality, for the reality of your mind is the loveliest of God's creations. Coming only from God, its power and grandeur could only bring you peace *if you really looked upon it*. If you are afraid, it is because you saw something that is not there. Yet in that same place you could have looked upon me and all your brothers, in the perfect safety of the Mind which created us. For we are there in the peace of the Father, Who wills to extend His peace through you.

Chapter 12 VII: 10 (1-6)

Grandeur is of God, and only of Him. Therefore it is in you: Whenever you become aware of it, however dimly, you abandon the ego automatically, because in the presence of the grandeur of God the meaninglessness of the ego becomes perfectly apparent. When this occurs, even though it does not understand it, the ego believes that its "enemy" has struck, and attempts to offer gifts to induce you to return to its "protection." Self-inflation is the only offering it can make. The grandiosity of the ego is its alternative to the grandeur of God. Which will you choose?

Chapter 9 VIII: 1 (1-7)

The ego depends solely on your willingness to tolerate it. If you are willing to look upon your grandeur you cannot despair, and therefore you cannot want the ego. Your grandeur is God's answer to the ego, because it is true.

Chapter 9 VIII: 6 (1-3)

If you remain as God created you, appearances cannot replace the truth, health cannot turn to sickness, nor can death be substituted for life, or fear for love. All this has not occurred, if you remain as God created you. You need no thought but just this one, to let redemption come to light the world and free it from the past.

In this one thought is all the past undone; the present saved to quietly extend into a timeless future. If you are as God created you, then there has been no separation of your mind from His, no split between your mind and other minds, and only unity within your own.

Workbook Lesson 110: 3 (1-3), 4 (1-2)

Seek Him within you Who is Christ in you, the Son of God and brother to the world; the Savior Who has been forever saved, with power to save whoever touches Him, however lightly, asking for the Word that tells him he is brother unto Him.

You are as God created you. Today honor your Self. Let graven images you made to be the Son of God instead of what he is be worshipped not today. Deep in your mind the holy Christ in you is waiting your acknowledgment as you. And you are lost and do not know yourself while He is unacknowledged and unknown.

Seek Him today, and find Him. He will be your Savior from all idols you have made. For when you find Him, you will understand how worthless are your idols, and how false the images which you believed were you. Today we make a great advance to truth by letting idols go, and opening our hands and hearts and minds to God today.

We will remember Him throughout the day with thankful hearts and loving thoughts for all who meet with us today. For it is thus that we remember Him. And we will say, that we may be reminded of His Son, our holy Self, the Christ in each of us:

I am as God created me.

Workbook Lesson 110: 8, 9, 10, 11

Miracles

To you the miracle cannot seem natural, because what you have done to hurt your mind has made it so unnatural that it does not remember what is natural to it. And when you are told what is natural, you cannot understand it. The recognition of the part as whole, and of the whole in every part is perfectly natural, for it is the way God thinks, and what is natural to Him is natural to you. Wholly natural perception would show you instantly that order of difficulty in miracles is quite impossible, for it involves a contradiction of what miracles mean. And if you could understand their meaning, their attributes could hardly cause you perplexity.

Chapter 16 II: 3 (1-5)

The miracle is means to demonstrate that all appearances can change because they *are* appearances, and cannot have the changelessness reality entails. The miracle attests salvation from appearances by showing they can change. Your brother has a changelessness in him beyond appearance and deception, both. It is obscured by changing views of him that you perceive as his reality. The happy dream about him takes the form of the appearance of his perfect health, his perfect freedom from all forms of lack, and safety from disaster of all kinds. The miracle is proof he is not bound by loss or suffering in any form, because it can so easily be changed. This demonstrates that it was never real, and could not stem from his reality. For that is changeless, and has no effects that anything in Heaven or on earth could ever alter. But appearances are shown to be unreal *because* they change.

Chapter 30 VIII: 2 (1-9)

Reality is changeless. Miracles but show what you have interposed between reality and your awareness is unreal, and does not interfere at all. The cost of belief there must be some appearances beyond the hope of change is that the miracle cannot come forth from you consistently. For you have asked it be withheld from power to heal all dreams. There is no miracle you cannot have when you desire healing. But there is no miracle that can be given you unless you want it. Choose what you would heal, and He Who gives all miracles has not been given freedom to bestow His gifts upon God's Son.

Chapter 30 VIII: 4 (1-7)

The miracle establishes you dream a dream, and that its content is not true. This is a crucial step in dealing with illusions. No one is afraid of them when he perceives he made them up. The fear was held in place because he did not see that he was author of the dream, and not a figure in the dream.

Chapter 28 II: 7 (1-4)

The miracle returns the cause of fear to you who made it. But it also shows that, having no effects, it is not cause, because the function of causation is to have effects. And where effects are gone, there is no cause. Thus is the body healed by miracles because they show the mind made sickness, and employed the body to be victim, or effect, of what it made. Yet half the lesson will not teach the whole. The miracle is useless if you learn but that the body can be healed, for this is not the lesson it was sent to teach. The lesson is the *mind* was sick that thought the body could be sick; projecting out its guilt caused nothing, and had no effects.

Chapter 28 II: 11 (1-7)

This world is full of miracles. They stand in shining silence next to every dream of pain and suffering, of sin and guilt. They are the dream's alternative, the choice to be the dreamer, rather than deny the active role in making up the dream.

Chapter 28 II: 12 (1-3)

Seek and *find* His message in the holy instant, where all illusions are forgiven. From there the miracle extends to bless everyone and to resolve all problems, be they perceived as great or small, possible or impossible. There is nothing that will not give place to Him and to His Majesty.

Chapter 16 VII: 11 (1-3)

Healing

Do not accept your brother's variable perception of himself for his split mind is yours, and you will not accept your healing without his. For you share the real world as you share Heaven, and his healing is yours. To love yourself is to heal yourself, and you cannot perceive part of you as sick and achieve your goal. Brother, we heal together as we live together and love together. Be not deceived in God's Son, for he is one with himself and one with his Father. Love him who is beloved of his Father, and you will learn of the Father's Love for you.

Chapter 11 VIII: 11 (1-6)

Every situation, properly perceived, becomes an opportunity to heal the Son of God. And he is healed *because* you offered faith to him, giving him to the Holy Spirit and releasing him from every demand your ego would make of him. Thus do you see him free, and in this vision does the Holy Spirit share. And since He shares it He has given it, and so He heals through you. It is this joining Him in a united purpose that makes this purpose real, because you make it whole. And this *is* healing. The body is healed because you came without it, and joined the Mind in which all healing rests.

Chapter 19 I: 2 (1-7)

The world obeys the laws that sickness serves, but healing operates apart from them. It is impossible that anyone be healed alone. In sickness must he be apart and separate. But healing is his own decision to be one again, and to accept his Self with all Its parts intact and unassailed. In sickness does his Self appear to be dismembered, and without the unity that gives It life. But healing is accomplished as he sees the body has no power to attack the universal Oneness of God's Son.

Workbook Lesson 137: 3 (1-6)

Sickness would prove that lies must be the truth. But healing demonstrates that truth is true. The separation sickness would impose has never really happened. To be healed is merely to accept what always was the simple truth, and always will remain exactly as it has forever been. Yet eyes accustomed to illusions must be shown that what they look upon is false. So healing, never needed by the truth, must demonstrate that sickness is not real.

Workbook Lesson 137: 4 (1-6)

Healing might thus be called a counter-dream, which cancels out the dream of sickness in the name of truth, but not in truth itself. Just as forgiveness overlooks all sins that never were accomplished, healing but removes illusions that have not occurred. Just as the real world will arise to take the place of what has never been at all, healing but offers restitution for imagined states and false ideas which dreams embroider into pictures of the truth.

Workbook Lesson 137: 5 (1-3)

Healing is freedom. For it demonstrates that dreams will not prevail against the truth. Healing is shared. And by this attribute it proves that laws unlike the ones which hold that sickness is inevitable are more potent than their sickly opposites. Healing is strength. For by its gentle hand is weakness overcome, and minds that were walled off within a body free to join with other minds, to be forever strong.

Workbook Lesson 137: 8 (1-6)

And as you let yourself be healed, you see all those around you, or who cross your mind, or whom you touch or those who seem to have no contact with you, healed along with you. Perhaps you will not recognize them all, nor realize how great your offering to all the world, when you let healing come to you. But you are never healed alone. And legions upon legions will receive the gift that you receive when you are healed.

Workbook Lesson 137: 10 (1-4)

Those who are healed become the instruments of healing. Nor does time elapse between the instant they are healed, and all the grace of healing it is given them to give. What is opposed to God does not exist, and who accepts it not within his mind becomes a haven where the weary can remain to rest. For here is truth bestowed, and here are all illusions brought to truth.

Workbook Lesson 137: 11 (1- 4)

Peace be to you who have been cured in God, and not in idle dreams. For cure must come from holiness, and holiness can not be found where sin is cherished. God abides in holy temples. He is barred where sin has entered. Yet there is no place where He is not. And therefore sin can have no home in which to hide from His beneficence. There is no place where holiness is not, and nowhere sin and sickness can abide.

Workbook Lesson 140: 5 (1-7)

Under the dusty edge of its distorted world the ego would lay the Son of God, slain by its orders, proof in his decay that God Himself is powerless before the ego's might, unable to protect the life that He created against the ego's savage wish to kill. My brother, child of our Father, this is a *dream* of death. There is no funeral, no dark altars, no grim commandments nor twisted rituals of condemnation to which the body leads you. Ask not release of *it*. But free it from the merciless and unrelenting orders you laid upon it, and forgive it what you ordered it to do. In its exaltation you commanded it to die, for only death could conquer life. And what but insanity could look upon the defeat of God, and think it real?

Chapter 19 IV: 8 (1-7)

The "self" that needs protection is not real. The body, valueless and hardly worth the least defense, need merely be perceived as quite apart from you, and it becomes a healthy, serviceable instrument through which the mind can operate until its usefulness is over. Who would want to keep it when its usefulness is done?

Workbook Lesson 135: 8 (1-3)

The Holy Relationship

The holy relationship, a major step toward the perception of the real world, is learned. It is the old, unholy relationship, transformed and seen anew. The holy relationship is a phenomenal teaching accomplishment. In all its aspects, as it begins, develops and becomes accomplished, it represents the reversal of the unholy relationship. Be comforted in this; the only difficult phase is the beginning. For here, the goal of the relationship is abruptly shifted to the exact opposite of what it was. This is the first result of offering the relationship to the Holy Spirit to use for His purposes.

Chapter 17 V: 2 (1-7)

This is the time for *faith*. You let this goal be set for you. That was an act of faith. Do not abandon faith, now that the rewards of faith are being introduced. If you believed the Holy Spirit was there to accept the relationship, why would you now not still believe that He is there to purify what He has taken under His guidance? Have faith in your brother in what but seems to be a trying time. The goal *is* set. And your relationship has sanity as its purpose.

Chapter 17 V: 6 (1-8)

The ego seeks to "resolve" its problems, not at their source, but where they were not made. And thus it seeks to guarantee there will be no solution. The Holy Spirit wants only to make His resolutions complete and perfect, and so He seeks and finds the source of problems where it is, and there undoes it. And with each step in His undoing is the separation more and more undone, and union brought closer. He is not at all confused by any "reasons" for separation. All He perceives in separation is that it must be undone. Let Him uncover the hidden spark of beauty in your relationships, and show it to you. Its loveliness will so attract you that you will be unwilling ever to lose sight of it again. And you will let this spark transform the relationship so you can see it more and more. For you will want it more and more, and become increasingly unwilling to let it be hidden from you. And you will learn to seek for and establish the conditions in which this beauty can be seen.

Chapter 17 III: 6 (1-11)

The special relationship is your determination to keep your hold on unreality, and to prevent yourself from waking. And while you see more value in sleeping than in waking, you will not let go of it.

The Holy Spirit, ever practical in His wisdom, accepts your dreams and uses them as means for waking. You would have used them to remain asleep. I said before that the first change, before dreams disappear, is that your dreams of fear are changed to happy dreams. That is what the Holy Spirit does in the holy relationship. He does not destroy it, nor snatch it away from you. But He does use it differently, as a help to make His purpose real to you. The special relationship will remain, not as a source of pain and guilt, but as a source of joy and freedom. It will not be for you alone, for therein lay its misery. As its unholiness kept it a thing apart, its holiness will become an offering to everyone.

Chapter 18 II: 5 (19-20), 6 (1-9)

Be sure of this; love has entered your special relationship, and entered fully at your weak request. You do not recognize that love has come, because you have not yet let go of all the barriers you hold against your brother. And you and he will not be able to give love welcome separately. You could no more know God alone than He knows you without your brother. But together you could no more be unaware of love than love could know you not, or fail to recognize itself in you.

Chapter 18 VIII: 12 (1-5)

You have reached the end of an ancient journey, not realizing yet that it is over. You are still worn and tired, and the desert's dust still seems to cloud your eyes and keep you sightless. Yet He Whom you welcomed has come to you, and would welcome you. He has waited long to give you this. Receive it now of Him, for He would have you know Him. Only a little wall of dust still stands between you and your brother. Blow on it lightly and with happy laughter, and it will fall away. And walk into the garden love has prepared for both of you.

Chapter 18 VIII: 13 (1-8)

Peace

When you have accepted your mission to extend peace you will find peace, for by making it manifest you will see it. Its holy witnesses will surround you because you called upon them, and they will come to you. I have heard your call and I have answered it, but you will not look upon me nor hear the answer that you sought. That is because you do not yet want *only* that. Yet as I become more real to you, you will learn that you do want only that. And you will see me as you look within, and we will look upon the real world together.

Chapter 12 VII: 11 (1-6)

Mistake not truce for peace, nor compromise for the escape from conflict. To be released from conflict means that it is over. The door is open; you have left the battleground. You have not lingered there in cowering hope that it will not return because the guns are stilled an instant, and the fear that haunts the place of death is not apparent. There *is* no safety in the battleground. You can look down on it in safety from above and not be touched. But from within it you can find no safety.

Chapter 23 III: 6 (1-7)

The peace of God is shining in you now, and from your heart extends around the world. It pauses to caress each living thing, and leaves a blessing with it that remains forever and forever. What it gives must be eternal. It removes all thoughts of the ephemeral and valueless. It brings renewal to all tired hearts, and lights all vision as it passes by. All of its gifts are given everyone, and everyone unites in giving thanks to you who give, and you who have received.

Workbook Lesson 188: 3 (1-6)

The peace of God can never be contained. Who recognizes it within himself must give it. And the means for giving it are in his understanding. He forgives because he recognized the truth in him. The peace of God is shining in you now, and in all living things. In quietness is it acknowledged universally. For what your inward vision looks upon is your perception of the universe.

Workbook Lesson 188: 5 (1-7)

Sit quietly and close your eyes. The light within you is sufficient. It alone has power to give the gift of sight to you. Exclude the outer world, and let your thoughts fly to the peace within. They know the way. For honest thoughts, untainted by the dream of worldly things outside yourself, become the holy messengers of God Himself.

These thoughts you think with Him. They recognize their home. And they point surely to their Source, Where God the Father and the Son are one.

Workbook Lesson 188: 6 (1-6), 7 (1-3)

Seek you no further. You will not find peace except the peace of God. Accept this fact, and save yourself the agony of yet more bitter disappointments, bleak despair, and sense of icy hopelessness and doubt. Seek you no further. There is nothing else for you to find except the peace of God, unless you seek for misery and pain.

Workbook Lesson 200: 1 (1-5)

Peace is the bridge that everyone will cross, to leave this world behind. But peace begins within the world perceived as different, and leading from this fresh perception to the gate of Heaven and the way beyond. Peace is the answer to conflicting goals, to senseless journeys, frantic, vain pursuits, and meaningless endeavors. Now the way is easy, sloping gently toward the bridge where freedom lies within the peace of God.

Workbook Lesson 200: 8 (1-4)

"I rest in God." This thought will bring to you the rest and quiet, peace and stillness, and the safety and the happiness you seek. "I rest in God." This thought has power to wake the sleeping truth in you, whose vision sees beyond appearances to that same truth in everyone and everything there is. Here is the end of suffering for all the world, and everyone who ever came and yet will come to linger for a while. Here is the thought in which the Son of God is born again, to recognize himself.

Workbook Lesson 109: 2 (1-6)

How instantly the memory of God arises in the mind that has no fear to keep the memory away! Its own remembering has gone. There is no past to keep its fearful image in the way of glad awakening to present peace. The trumpets of eternity resound throughout the stillness, yet disturb it not. And what is now remembered is not fear, but rather is the Cause that fear was made to render unremembered and undone. The stillness speaks in gentle sounds of love the Son of God remembers from before his own remembering came in between the present and the past, to shut them out.

Chapter 28 I: 13 (1-6)

And when the memory of God has come to you in the holy place of forgiveness you will remember nothing else, and memory will be as useless as learning, for your only purpose will be creating. Yet this you cannot know until every perception has been cleansed and purified, and finally removed forever. Forgiveness removes only the untrue, lifting the shadows from the world and carrying it, safe and sure within its gentleness, to the bright world of new and clean perception. There is your purpose *now*. And it is there that peace awaits you.

Chapter 18 IX: 14 (1-5)

The End of Perception

Into Christ's Presence will we enter now, serenely unaware of everything except His shining face and perfect Love. The vision of His face will stay with you, but there will be an instant which transcends all vision, even this, the holiest. This you will never teach, for you attained it not through learning. Yet the vision speaks of your remembrance of what you knew that instant, and will surely know again.

Workbook Lesson 157: 9 (1-4)

Oneness is simply the idea God is. And in His Being, He encompasses all things. No mind holds anything but Him. We say "God is," and then we cease to speak, for in that knowledge words are meaningless. There are no lips to speak them, and no part of mind sufficiently distinct to feel that it is now aware of something not itself. It has united with its Source. And like its Source Itself, it merely is.

We cannot speak nor write nor even think of this at all. It comes to every mind when total recognition that its will is God's has been completely given and received completely. It returns the mind into the endless present, where the past and future cannot be conceived. It lies beyond salvation; past all thought of time, forgiveness and the holy face of Christ. The Son of God has merely disappeared into his Father, as his Father has in him. The world has never been at all. Eternity remains a constant state.

Workbook Lesson 169: 5 (1-7), 6 (1-7)

The very real difference between perception and knowledge becomes quite apparent if you consider this: There is nothing partial about knowledge. Every aspect is whole, and therefore no aspect is separate. You are an aspect of knowledge, being in the Mind of God, Who knows you. All knowledge must be yours, for in you is all knowledge. Perception, at its loftiest, is never complete. Even the perception of the Holy Spirit, as perfect as perception can be, is without meaning in Heaven. Perception can reach everywhere under His guidance, for the vision of Christ beholds everything in light. Yet no perception, however holy, will last forever.

Chapter 13 VIII: 2 (1-8)

Perfect perception, then, has many elements in common with knowledge, making transfer to it possible. Yet the last step must be taken by God, because the last step in your redemption, which seems to be in the future, was accomplished by God in your creation. The separation has not interrupted it. Creation cannot be interrupted. The separation is merely a faulty formulation of reality, with no effect at all. The miracle, without a function in Heaven, is needful here. Aspects of reality can still be seen, and they will replace aspects of unreality. Aspects of reality can be seen in everything and everywhere. Yet only God can gather them together, by crowing them as one with the final gift of eternity.

Chapter 13 VIII: 3 (1-9)

Christ's Second Coming, which is sure as God, is merely the correction of mistakes, and the return of sanity. It is a part of the condition that restores the never lost, and re-establishes what is forever and forever true. It is the invitation to God's Word to take illusion's place; the willingness to let forgiveness rest upon all things without exception and without reserve.

Workbook: What Is the Second Coming? 1 (1-3)

The Second Coming ends the lessons that the Holy Spirit teaches, making way for the Last Judgment, in which learning ends in one last summary that will extend beyond itself, and reaches up to God. The Second coming is the time in which all minds are given to the hands of Christ, to be returned to spirit in the name of true creation and the Will of God.

The Second Coming is the one event in time which time itself can not affect. For every one who ever came to die, or yet will come or who is present now, is equally released from what he made. In this equality is Christ restored as one Identity, in which the Sons of God acknowledge that they all are one. And God the Father smiles upon His Son, His one creation and His only Joy.

Workbook: What Is the Second Coming? 3 (1-2), 4 (1-4)

Christ's Second Coming gives the Son of God this gift: to hear the Voice for God proclaim that what is false is false, and what is true has never changed. And this the judgment is in which perception ends. At first you see a world that has accepted this as true, projected from a now corrected mind. And with this holy sight, perception gives a silent blessing and then disappears, its goal accomplished and its mission done.

The final judgment on the world contains no condemnation. For it sees the world as totally forgiven, without sin and wholly purposeless. Without a cause, and now without a function in Christ's sight, it merely slips away to nothingness. There it was born, and there it ends as well. And all the figures in the dream in which the world began go with it. Bodies now are useless, and will therefore fade away, because the Son of God is limitless.

You who believed that God's Last Judgment would condemn the world to hell along with you, accept this holy truth: God's Judgment is the gift of the Correction He bestowed on all your errors, freeing you from them, and all effects they ever seemed to have. To fear God's saving grace is but to fear complete release from suffering, return to peace, security and happiness, and union with your own Identity.

Workbook: What Is the Last Judgment? 1(1-4), 2 (1-6), 3 (1-2)

There are no hidden chambers in God's temple. Its gates are open wide to greet His Son. No one can fail to come where God has called him, if he close not the door himself upon his Father's welcome.

Chapter 14 VI: 8 (6-8)

This is God's Final Judgment: "You are still My holy Son, forever innocent, forever loving and forever loved, as limitless as your Creator, and completely changeless and forever pure. Therefore awaken and return to Me. I am your Father and you are My Son."

Workbook: What Is the Last Judgment? 5 (1-3)

Epilogue

Having concluded *The Door Held Open*, it is my genuine hope that you found encouragement and even joy in these pages. I smile inwardly in the thought of those who will return here often, and to the pages of *A Course in Miracles*, finding inspiration and useful instruction.

As is the case with any spiritual teaching and any written text, the *Course* has been, and will continue to be, quoted and interpreted by a great variety of people, all of whom will not be in agreement as to its meaning or its message for humanity. It goes without saying that there will be students and teachers alike, who offer interpretations and so-called meanings that lack both accuracy and depth. There will be those who once again miss the point; only this time they've got a copy of *A Course in Miracles* tucked underneath their arm. None of this is anything new, and all of it just presents us with opportunities to practice what we preach in terms of forgiveness. It's far too easy to allow someone else's "wrongness" to become the arrogant basis of our own self-proclaimed "rightness." That being said, I feel compelled to clarify a point which often causes confusion and misunderstanding.

The notion that the world *as we see it* is our own projection can raise a fair amount of doubt and consternation, and is just the kind of thing that keeps many a philosopher up at night. The key here lies in the "as we see it" part. Reality is not the projection of any individual. God's Will is forever the *only* reality. However, each individual's perception is totally governed by what is projected from within. Our perception of the world is a reflection of what we think we see within us. Hand in hand with this principle is the idea that healing can occur through one's accepting of what the *Course* calls the Atonement; the Correction of the original mistake of separation. In Atonement and in healing, which are identical, the reality of God's Presence totally replaces the illusion of separation and also dissolves illusion's painful effects, simply because in the face of truth, illusion can not exist and so can have no effects. This is the hidden and glorious underbelly of every miracle. There are unfortunately, some who misunderstand and, I feel, misrepresent the true significance of this teaching. This happens when the core understanding that we are One is not kept clearly in mind. If we fail to acknowledge our Oneness, losing sight of the face of Christ, what has been written and offered as the freeing Word of God can come off sounding aloof, naive, and even heartless. Catchy little nuggets of New-Age-speak are not what's called for in the face of chaos and calamity. We should never let anyone feel removed or apart from us in their suffering or sorrow. Rather we should join with them *deeper* than their pain has allowed them to see. We all abide as One in the Heart of God. Meet your brothers and sisters There, not leaving them alone and wounded on the field of conflict, *nor* accepting their wounds as the truth of the situation. The truth is always our Unity in Love; the eternal Oneness that is our real and shared Identity.

Following are two passages that present a beautiful and clear statement as to how we should live in this world, even as we awaken together beyond it. In Chapter 26 we read, "Abide in peace, where God would have you be. And be the means whereby your brother finds the peace in which your wishes are fulfilled. Let us unite in bringing blessing to the world of sin and death. For what can save each one of us can save us all. There is no difference among the Sons of God. The unity that specialness denies will save them all, for what is one can have no specialness. And everything belongs to each of them. No wishes lie between a brother and his own. To get from one is to deprive them all. And yet to bless but one gives blessing to them all as one." Finally, Workbook Lesson 109 offers us this statement and pledge, "You rest within the peace of God today, and call upon your brothers from your rest to draw them to their rest, along with you. You will be faithful to your trust today, forgetting no one, bringing everyone into the boundless circle of your peace, the holy sanctuary where you rest. Open the temple doors and let them come from far across the world, and near as well; your distant brothers and your closest friends; bid them all enter here and rest with you."

About the Author

John Cornell has been a student of sacred texts and a practitioner of meditation for over thirty-five years. This study and practice ultimately led him to regard the teachings of Non-duality, or absolute oneness, as representing the very deepest expression of wisdom. To his great joy and amazement, this same uncompromising Non-dualism was found to be at the core of *A Course in Miracles*. This discovery began a journey that led to the writing of *The Door Held Open,* and that continues to this day.